COOK *the* PART™

DELICIOUS, INTERACTIVE *and fun* TEAM COOKING

COOK *the* PART™

DELICIOUS, INTERACTIVE *and fun* TEAM COOKING

KARIN EASTHAM

illustrations by
TRACI O'VERY COVEY

photography by
CARI LIGHTFOOT PIKE

Visit my website: www.cookthepart.com.   Join my network: www.facebook.com/cookthepart.

Follow me on twitter @cookthepart.

. . . .

Karin Eastham
Copyright © 2011 Karin Eastham
Illustrations copyright © 2011 Traci O'Very Covey

Crosswalk Press LLC
P.O. Box 928723
San Diego, CA 92192-8723
www.crosswalkpress.com
info@crosswalkpress.com

Publisher's Cataloging-in-Publication data

Eastham, Karin.
    Cook the part : delicious, interactive, and fun team cooking / Karin Eastham.
    p. cm.
    ISBN 978-0-9845563-2-8

1. Cooking. 2. Dinners and dining. 3. Entertaining. 4. International cooking. 5. Menus. 6. Teams in the workplace. I. Title.

TX737 .E37 2011
641.5/4 –dc22

Printed in the United States
Carr Printing Co.
Bountiful, UT

Designed and produced by: Traci O'Very Covey
Photography: Cari Lightfoot Pike   Lighting Director: Will McGarry
Contributing Photographer: Karin Eastham

TABLE OF
contents

on the menu

DEDICATION

This book is dedicated to my mother, Irmgard Froehlich, who instilled in me a love for cooking and enjoyment of food with friends and family. Through the example of her warm hospitality and generosity, we have been able to enjoy many special occasions with our guests, learning the true meaning of *Gemütlichkeit*.

❧ ❧ ❧

ACKNOWLEDGMENTS

I want to express my love and gratitude to my wonderfully creative and very patient husband and cooking partner, Gary. This book could not have been written without his advice, guidance, infinite wisdom and many inspired recipe contributions.

My two children, Eric and Kristina, deserve special thanks for their unwavering love, support and enthusiasm for my project. To Eric, for providing legal guidance on my copyright and trademark issues, while also contributing to the development of the *Pacific Northwest Seafood Evening* chapter, one of my favorites. And to my lovely and high-spirited daughter, Kristina, who encouraged me to "just do it, Mom," from the first day that I mentioned the idea of writing this book. Her knowledge and expertise in social media and online marketing helped promote *Cook the Part* as she established my blog (www.cookthepart.com), my Facebook page (www.facebook.com/cookthepart), and my Twitter account (@cookthepart), and gave me "suggested quotas" for content. Much love to both of you and many thanks for your inspiration.

I also owe a debt of gratitude to the following dear friends and advisors who helped me stay true to creating a book that not only extolls the virtues of "team cooking," but also shows people how to have fun while creating a great dinner together.

Gloria Robbins, my friend and sounding board, who rallied behind me when I most needed it, and laughed with me when I most needed it.

Barbara Zaugg, one of my editors and a dear friend who tirelessly cooked with me, made sound suggestions and recommendations, and helped to ensure a quality manuscript.

Lise Zondler, award-winning baker and frequent contributor to my blog, who helped test many of the chapters in this book.

Rhonda Rhyne and Bryna Kranzler, my publishing partners, who guided me through the publishing process and became invaluable members of my team.

Bobi Lindeborg and JoAnn Gayer, who helped with the creation of the manuscript and the original layout of recipes and plans.

Traci O'Very Covey, amazingly talented creative director, graphic designer, illustrator, and now a friend, who helped make this book a work of art.

Also special thanks to Cari Lightfoot Pike, photographer, and Will McGarry, lighting director, whose artistry so perfectly captured the essence of well-prepared food and good friends coming together to prepare a great meal and enjoy each other's company.

And finally, to all of you who have joined us in our home to *Cook the Part,* or hosted an event in your own homes: Thank you for being part of this incredible journey.

INTRODUCTION
a new team cooking experience

Ready to experience a new twist on entertaining? *Cook the Part* is much more than a collection of recipes. It's an entertaining revolution. Each of the eight themed menus in this book is divided into "parts," so that your guests work in teams to cook part of a fabulous four-course meal. *Cook the Part* shows you how to organize and create a memorable evening of hands-on cooking while enjoying the camaraderie of your guests and a phenomenal gourmet dinner.

If you are intimidated by the thought of hosting a dinner party, let this book boost your confidence. *Cook the Part* allows anyone, even the inexperienced cook, to host dinner parties that will leave guests talking for months. The secret ingredient to your success is the perfect plan. Each of the eight themed menus is divided into four parts for four teams, designated as teams A, B, C and D, and offers organized step-by-step instructions for each team.

Some of the recipes in this book are family favorites, while others were created specifically for the book and also to satisfy the global palette. Indeed, prepare the Spanish paella to pique your passion; see how the Greek souvlaki satisfies your soul; and feel how the fish tacos fire your feisty side. Experience the power of team cooking as your guests become energized by the work and enthusiasm of fellow cooks and are amazed to realize they actually possess the cooking skills to create these dishes. Eight to twelve cooks can accomplish so much more in a few hours than you could over the course of days or even a full week of advance preparation. Enjoy each hour in the kitchen to the fullest as you bond, reconnect and feast with those special people in your life.

In addition to providing step-by-step instructions for teams to create sumptuous dishes, this book also focuses on the entertainment aspect of your evening. Of course you are creating a memorable meal, but more importantly, you are creating a memorable experience. By interacting on a fun and satisfying novel level, new friendships are formed, old friendships are solidified and a great time is had by all!

WHY I WROTE THIS BOOK

My love for cooking and good food was established early in life. I grew up in a German immigrant household near Chicago, in which my mother, *Mutti* (German for mom), constantly cooked for friends and relatives. As a young girl, I was often summoned to help prepare grand dinners and desserts, assisting my mother in making sure that home-cooked food was always available—even for unexpected guests. *Mutti's* cooking was so exceptional that my father refused to eat in restaurants. For my wedding in 1968, *Mutti* prepared all the food for over 150 guests, hiring only a few helpers to finish the preparation and serve dinner. The wedding cake came from a traditional bakery, but *Mutti* supplemented the desserts with multiple homemade German tortes, some filled with mocha buttercream and others with her homemade raspberry jam. These beautifully prepared tortes were so inviting that, on the wedding night, they tempted a torte thief: two tortes were stolen from the kitchen during the reception. The mystery remains unsolved to this day.

During my childhood, I often worked side by side with unannounced visitors who were put to work when they entered the domain ruled by *Mutti*. She was a real delegator and teacher. I still remember *Mutti* barking orders at us while she tried to multitask as stovetop and oven-baked creations competed for her attention. Her guests always came back for more—the food and the work—because they enjoyed learning, creating and indulging.

LEFT: A typical scene in the kitchen of Irma Froehlich (*Mutti*), gourmet cook.

RIGHT: Irma and my sister, Erika, cleaning bushels of mushrooms picked in an Indiana forest. Irma was known by her friends as the "Mushroom Queen."

Many of my fondest memories, from childhood through adulthood, revolve around experiences shared in the kitchen, cooking with friends and family. When I smell specific foods, I am "whisked" away to kitchens of my past.

I also share this love of cooking with my husband, Gary, our children and our extended family. Each year we host many cooking events in our home, including a week-long Thanksgiving feast. The kitchen becomes the primary gathering place as we drink wine, play music and dance to everything from Motown to Disco. Throughout the week, guests are assigned tasks that contribute to a wonderful outcome on the big day. Attendees vary from year to year, but my cousin Helen, her husband, Sam, and their three adult children, return annually, having been raised with the same love of cooking through our shared heritage.

Over the years, specific responsibilities have evolved. Sam always chops the vegetables. Helen always preps the turkeys. My husband, Gary, gets up at 4 AM to start the smoker. My daughter-in-law, Maria, a kindergarten teacher, always makes creative place cards; and my son, Eric, always mashes the potatoes. Everyone does his or her part to contribute to the incredible meal that follows. The joy we share in cooking is rivaled only by the satisfaction of enjoying the fruits of our labor at the dinner table.

As a gourmet food enthusiast, I have also participated in many cooking and dining groups in the Midwest and in California. While the friends and cuisine have changed over the years, I discovered that the one constant is the need for better organization. Organization is of utmost importance in the kitchen to ensure a perfect outcome. Otherwise, it's easy to forget to put sugar in the pumpkin pie or to miss an entire dish that is discovered in the oven during clean-up. Or, the main dish grows cold while waiting for the accompanying dishes to finish cooking. Too often, guests are left standing around wondering how they can help, while the hosts scramble from one task to the next, too harried to stop and figure out what to delegate.

The success of our Thanksgiving cooking plan inspired me to try other cooking adventures. It started with pasta making. A group of friends who love to cook decided to get together for a "Pasta Fest." I offered our kitchen. We decided to make multiple forms of pasta and multiple sauces. How could you possibly tackle this with twelve people without a plan? My planning started with the end-goal in sight, and I gave assignments to each couple for what to bring and what to do. It was perfect harmony as we all enjoyed the afternoon making dough, cutting linguini, drying the pasta over broom handles and stirring our sauces. It was delightful and delicious. All of the guests really appreciated the "cheat sheets" so that they could "cook their part" without constantly nagging the chef, asking "what can I do next?"

This was the beginning of the concept for this book. Why not provide a guide to hosts who love to cook and eat? I decided to try it out and created my first menu—the *Tuscan Farmhouse Dinner*. Most of the recipes in this menu, created by Gary, are tried and true. We documented our recipes, and I divided the work into parts for eight guests. Then we tried it out with multiple groups of friends. We knew it was a hit when they all wanted to come back the following weekend and try it again with a different menu.

Since then, new themes, new menus, new recipes and new experiences with friends have further refined our concept. We have had so much fun in the process. Some of my best friendships have been formed with "cooking buddies," some of whom were experienced cooks while others were complete novices.

Cook the Part applies principles of teamwork, delegation, mentoring and project planning to the art of cooking. You do not have to be an experienced chef to tackle one of these menus. While these are gourmet recipes, they are broken down into simple steps. Each guest lends a hand and works toward the common culinary goal. The more experienced cooks can provide guidance to the novices, who increase their culinary confidence and knowledge in the kitchen in a fun, relaxed environment.

Embark on eight different culinary adventures, but tackle the menus multiple times with different guests. Each experience will be unique as different challenges and rewards emerge. As your guest list changes, so will your experience. Each adventure is guaranteed to create lasting memories. Get better acquainted with your guests, create fabulous meals and actually enjoy your next dinner party. Simply invite your guests to *Cook the Part*.

HERE'S THE WAY IT WORKS

Begin by making a guest list and choosing one of the themed menus. Once you decide on the menu and your guests, set the date and send out an enticing invitation. I find it helpful to assign the teams and to send a copy of the chapter to my guests in advance. Be sure to read the section entitled "Forming Teams" before you assign your guests to a team. You may copy the selected themed chapter from the book and provide a copy to each of your guests. Guests may want to take the time to read through the instructions before arriving at your party. Even if the instructions are sent to guests in advance, it is important for the host to review the instructions with all guests upon their arrival.

Carefully read through the recipes, the Master Plan and Team Plans for your selected menu before working on the details of your cooking party.

The Recipes: Each recipe is divided into numbered steps. Each step is assigned to either the Host or one of the Teams. The recipes provide all the detailed instructions.

The Team Plan: The Team Plan includes important information for the Host and each cooking Team. The Host will use the team plan to determine workstations required by each team (counter area, stovetop, etc.) The Host will also refer to the Team Plan to lay out cooking tools and ingredients for each team.

The Teams will follow the Team Plan, working on each of the recipe steps assigned to their team during the timeline indicated. The teams must follow the detailed instructions in the recipe, but refer to the Team Plan for timing and an overview of their assignments.

The Master Plan: The Master Plan provides information to the Host on the advance preparation required, both general and menu-specific. The Master Plan also provides an overview of all the assignments given to each team in each timeslot. It is the responsibility of the host to coordinate the final timing for each course by checking in with each team as the evening progresses.

planning your party

THE GUEST LIST

Start with your guest list. First, decide on the number of people in the group. The menus are designed for parties of eight, but can be easily be modified for six to twelve guests.

ADJUSTING THE NUMBER OF GUESTS

For a Smaller Cooking Group

To reduce the number of guests to six, simply take one of the Team Plans and divide the tasks among the other teams, taking into account the difficulty of each task and the timing. An alternative way to reduce the size of the group is for the hosts to complete the tasks for one of the teams in advance of the dinner (such as preparing the dessert), making it easy for all participants to absorb any last minute work. You can even reduce the size of the group to four, making each person responsible for the work of one team. Remember to reduce quantities where appropriate.

For a Larger Cooking Group

Increasing the number of guests is also relatively easy, but requires the hosts to adjust the quantities in the recipes. Many of the side dishes do not have to be increased, but most meat servings should be increased according to the number of guests. Large cakes can easily serve up to twelve people, but the individual desserts will have to be adjusted. Allow a bit of extra prep time if you increase the number of guests. Increase the size of each of the teams to three people instead of two people each. Because of workspace availability, it is difficult to adjust the number of guests beyond twelve and still cook together in most kitchens.

Another option is for hosts to serve as facilitators and not on a team. They can make sure to preheat ovens, clean up after the cooking teams, pour wine, and provide general guidance as the work progresses.

THE THEMED MENU

Once you decide on the guests, select a menu. The *Handmade Pasta with Homemade Sauces* is a wonderful team-building project for a group that works together. Or the theme can be linked to the time of year, a particular season or a special occasion. For example, *A Taste of Baja* might be great for a "Cinco de Mayo" party in early May, while *Comfort Food* is perfect during colder autumn or winter months. For a birthday celebration, simply select a favorite menu for the honored guest or give the guest a few choices.

RECIPE DIFFICULTY LEVEL

The menus and recipes focus on dishes with a broad contemporary appeal and a moderate level of cooking difficulty.

The menu chapters vary in difficulty, with the *Pacific Northwest Seafood Evening* and *A Taste of Baja* representing the easier chapters. The *Spanish Wine Dinner* chapter represent a more challenging menu.

The recipes in this book allow you to create very special gourmet meals, requiring only a reasonable time commitment by the host and guests.

Some of the menus include homemade breads. Don't let that intimidate you, at least not if you have a bread machine. When bread machines became a household appliance, we started cranking out focaccia and pizza dough with our own recipe variations. Now that these machines are no longer the craze, you can pick them up at consignment stores for $5 to $20. I recommend buying one to create the recipes in this book. With a bread machine, homemade bread takes minutes to prepare and adds a very special touch to the dinners that you will be creating.

Each menu includes a special dessert recipe that would likely intimidate an inexperienced home cook. In the team context, these recipes are much less complicated than you would imagine. The team approach enables you and your guests to feel comfortable experimenting with new techniques and kitchen tools. Teams can tackle homemade gelato or even "fallen" chocolate cakes.

ATTIRE

These dinners are designed to be casual evenings, with the focus being on the cooking as much as on the dining. Guide your guests to wear comfortable clothes and shoes,

as they will be standing in the kitchen and cooking. Also encourage each guest to bring an apron, unless you have enough aprons to go around. For special occasions where a gift is in order, consider giving aprons to your guests to mark the memorable event.

TIMING

All of the menus are designed to begin at 6 PM with the main course to be served within 2 or 2 ½ hours. This timing is only a guideline and can be adjusted by the host when you copy the Master Plan and Team Plan. Recognize also that teams will work at differing speeds, so these times are all very approximate.

THE INVITATION

Invitations can be sent via regular mail, but if you want to keep it simple, use email, an invitation website or a social networking site to notify invitees. Your guests need to know that they are being invited to *Cook the Part* and will play an important role in the evening. Check on the availability of your guests before sending them an invitation. Use the invitation to tell your guests to bring an apron and wear comfortable clothing. You can also include the entire menu chapter so guests can read the cooking plan and be more prepared for the evening. The invitation should inspire and entice, so send the menu. A sample follows.

. . . .

Dear Guest,

Please join us for a Tuscan Farmhouse Dinner.

You are invited to Cook the Part!

Please arrive between 5:30 and 6:00 p.m. Cooking will begin promptly at 6:00. Please bring your aprons and wear comfortable shoes and attire for the cooking process. Our menu follows:

Antipasto Platter
Insalata Caprese
Chicken Under a Brick
Tuscan White Beans
Grilled Zucchini
Fallen Chocolate Cakes

We will work in small groups, but create everything together. You do not need to be a chef to participate. Please come to enjoy the cooking experience and learn some new techniques from each other.

See you in the Eastham kitchen!
Gary and Karin Eastham

getting ready

To ensure a successful party, planning and advance preparation are crucial. The following sections will provide you with guidance for your planning.

CHOOSING INGREDIENTS

Review each of the recipes in your chosen menu. Next, gather available ingredients from your pantry and make your shopping list for the remaining items.

If you want to have an incredible meal, choose fresh, organic ingredients. Aside from the environmental and health benefits of organic ingredients, you will find the taste is far superior to standard fare. It costs a bit more, but the price is well worth the extra flavor. Don't forget, farmers markets are the best places to find the freshest local ingredients.

Always use vegetables that are in season. For example, a delicious summer option would be the Insalata Caprese in the *Tuscan Farmhouse Dinner*. You would not want to serve tomatoes in the middle of winter when, no matter how fresh, tomatoes are essentially tasteless. Instead, you would select the Bibb and Red Leaf Salad with Champagne Vinaigrette. For the fruit desserts, substitute in-season fruits for those called for in the recipes.

PREPARING THE TABLE

For the Tuscan, Baja or Athens dinners, use your most colorful dishes to create the right mood. If you have only white dishes, use tablecloths, napkins, runners, glassware, accent pieces, candle holders, serving pieces or flowers to provide color. You could even consider purchasing colorful salad plates and placing them on your white dinner plates for accent.

For very special parties, you may want to use your best china and crystal. When you use the best, consider rinsing dishes and leaving all crystal to be washed the next morning when all the wine effects have worn off. We have broken more than a few glasses when trying to do all the clean up after the dinner party.

After years of excessive spending on flowers for dinner parties, I learned that the best solution is to pick something from the yard or garden and supplement with a few purchased flowers. Small potted flowers in plastic pots can simply be placed inside of an interesting low vase or container. In colder climates, a few branches of cut evergreens from the yard can be supplemented with a few purchased flowers. This way you save your money for the star of the show—the food!

Set the table or prepare the table and lay out dishes for a buffet. Think about each course as you stage your dishes, including the coffee and dessert course. I recommend leaving dessert forks and coffee spoons in the staging area instead of placing them on the table in advance. That way, they are not accidentally cleared by a helpful guest before the dessert course.

All of the menus can be served buffet style or plated individually. You can vary the serving style for each course: plate the salad, but have guests be seated and then pass the main course family style. If you opt for buffet-style service, you will need additional space for serving—perhaps in the dining room, as the kitchen will be busy and somewhat messy when you are ready to dine.

Printing menu cards for each place setting adds a lot of class. Then everyone can take a card home to remember the evening and the special menu.

LABELING SERVING DISHES AND UTENSILS

Lay out serving dishes and utensils for each item in your menu. Put a Post-it note or index card on each serving piece so that the teams know which piece to use when things get hectic in the kitchen. Whether you serve the dinner family or buffet style will influence your choice of serving pieces, so you will have to make that decision early in your planning process. If you do not have enough serving pieces or particular kitchen tools, ask one of your guests to bring them along.

WORKSTATIONS

Work Space, Tools and Ingredients

Workstations should be set up for each team and labeled accordingly (Team A, B, C or D). Some equipment or ingredients will be shared by multiple teams. Lay out the appropriate tools for each of your teams. These workstations will be outlined in the Team Plan for each of the menus in this book. As you organize your workstations, use prep bowls with labels similar to those used on television cooking shows. If you do not prepare all the ingredients as called for in the recipe, you must provide the additional tools for guests to complete the process. (i.e., If a recipe calls for chopped onion, you have the option of placing the whole onion at a workstation, but must provide a cutting board and knife to allow your guest to prepare the ingredient.)

If your kitchen is small, you will need to be creative about workstations. You can put the grill team to work at an outside table in the summer, set up a card table for one team or use the kitchen table in addition to your kitchen counters. A crowded, busy kitchen adds to the fun and the excitement of creating the meal together.

BEVERAGES

Select your wines for each course and chill as appropriate. Have the appropriate glasses ready for use. Definitely use name tags or charms for the glasses so guests can keep track of their own glasses while they are cooking.

Ask one of the teams to fill water glasses approximately 15 minutes before the main course is to be served. A pitcher of ice water with lemon slices can be ready in the fridge. Alternatively, you may elect to serve sparkling water, which is best served chilled without ice.

APPETIZERS

Since your guests will be cooking for two or more hours before dinner is served, it is important to have appetizers ready or to have your teams prepare an easy appetizer upon arrival. The menus are designed with that objective in mind. Appetizers are designed to be on the light side, however, so as not to fill your guests too much before dinner.

COFFEE

Have the coffeemaker set to go so that you only have to hit the "on" button. Always offer real half-and-half with your coffee in addition to real sugar and artificial sweeteners. Most guests prefer decaf coffee late in the evening. If you have an espresso machine, offer lattes, cappuccinos or espresso shots as a wonderful conclusion to the meal.

when guests arrive

UPON ARRIVAL

The invitations ask guests to arrive between 5:30 and 6:00 PM so that you can go over the plans prior to cooking. Welcome them and offer them your selected wines or other beverages. Pour the drinks into the glasses that have been tagged with guest names. Serve the host-prepared appetizer or get guests involved in preparing the appetizers as described in some of the menus. I like to gather guests around a kitchen table or coffee table so that they can enjoy appetizers while I review the Guest Orientation with them. Even if some guests arrive late, start cooking on schedule so that your evening can remain on track.

FORMING TEAMS

Each of the menus is designed for four teams of two or three guests each. Try to pair a more experienced cook with a less experienced one. Ask your guests about their cooking skill level to help determine the best teams. It is best, as host, to assign yourself to one of the teams with a lighter load so that you can provide some oversight or assist with tools and ingredients, if necessary. Separate couples so guests can get better acquainted with each other and assign teams according to guests' strengths, i.e. my husband will always be on a team that is responsible for grilling since he is quite familiar with how to get the most out of the grill. If you have any bakers in the group, try to steer them to the team responsible for any baking, but then pair a novice baker with the master.

KEEP COOKING!

You and your guests will have so much fun that you may want to plan another dinner adventure together. You can even form a permanent group of couples who meet every month or so to enjoy another menu. Couples can take turns hosting the parties or sharing the costs.

You are invited to post comments about your *Cook the Part* events on my website (www.cookthepart.com), or my Facebook page (www.facebook.com/cookthepart). Enjoy creating special memories with your friends in your kitchen.

Here are a few quotes from guests who have attended recent *Cook the Part* events:

"The step-by-step, piece-by-piece, everybody's-got-a-role approach to meal preparation gives me the confidence to host a dinner party that I know will be fabulous and fun."

"I can't believe I actually made a chocolate soufflé … and it was easy!"

"I love the team concept, whether in sports or work, so I was glad to be so directly included in the food preparation."

"We all need to eat, but Cook the Part created a deep satisfaction in a job well done, together."

"Having everyone participate in preparing the meal was a bonding experience for the group. Everyone had a vested interest in the outcome of the gourmet meal we all shared. Good times, good food and laughter brought us together to 'Cook the Part' for a delightful evening of gourmet dining. Delicious, doable and a learning experience for an evening that flies by."

"What a fun way to spend an evening and a great way to get better acquainted with new friends and old."

"I never considered myself a master of the marinade and now I do."

"We feel like family now that we've cooked together."

HOST PREP
guidelines

- Make five copies of the chapter that you have chosen for your dinner: one copy for the host and 4 copies for the teams.
- Carefully review each of the recipes, noting any advance preparation required by the Host. While the "Host Preparation" page included in every chapter captures some of the more important advance prep requirements, you will need to review each chapter to ensure that you plan appropriately.
- Check your pantry for required spices and staples. Prepare your grocery list.
- Shop for your ingredients.
- Set your table and, if desired, your buffet table.
- Label all serving pieces and serving utensils and place them in a convenient location for teams to access.
- Label workstations (Team A, B, C or D). This will show each of your teams where they should work.
- Prepare four workstations with the tools, and ingredients required for each team. The party will work more smoothly if the host actually chops the ingredients as called for in the recipes and places them at the workstations.
- Label the ingredients if there is any question about the quantity placed in a prep bowl or the applicable recipe (i.e. ½ cup onion, chopped: Mexican Rice). Alternatively, you can put cutting boards, knives and measuring tools at each station (if not already included), but be sure to plan extra cooking time if you elect this option.
- Set up a coffee maker to be ready to brew after the main course is finished.
- Label wine glasses with name tags or charms.
- Open appropriate wines; prepare cocktails; prepare beverages.
- Set out host-prepared appetizers.
- Follow any additional instructions specific to each menu as summarized under "Host Preparation" on the Master Plan for each chapter.

GUEST
orientation

- Welcome guests and serve beverages as each of your guests arrive.
- Have guests put on their aprons as they arrive.
- Find a comfortable spot to gather and serve any host-prepared appetizers while you review this Guest Orientation.
- Select teams, if not done in advance.
- Give each team a copy of the menu chapter.
- Explain the use of Recipes, Team Plan, and Master Plan.
- **The Recipes:** Each recipe is divided into numbered steps. Each step is assigned to either the Host or one of the Teams. You and your guests must follow the recipes while you are cooking.
- **The Team Plan:** The Team Plan includes important information for the Host and the cooking Team. The Host will use the team plan to determine workstations required by each team (counter area, stovetop, etc.). The Host will also refer to the Team Plan to lay out cooking tools and ingredients for each team.

  The Teams will follow the Team Plan, working on each of the recipe steps assigned to their team during the timeline indicated. The teams must follow the detailed instructions in the recipe, but refer to the Team Plan for timing and an overview of their assignments.
- **The Master Plan:** The Master Plan provides information to the Host on preparation required, both general and menu-specific. The Master Plan also provides an overview of all the assignments given to each team in each timeslot.
- Review the Master Plan for this event with the group.
- Ask guests to read their Team Plan and each of their recipes to get an overview of their "part." This is very important!
- Tell guests where to find the serving pieces and any shared cooking tools.
- Ask guests not to clear the table of glasses as this is better done the next day.
- Direct guests to their workstations.
- Tell guests that you will check on progress for the main course to ensure that last minute tasks are completed and all dishes in the course are ready simultaneously. Because the Master Plan is only a guideline, direct the teams to coordinate with you on the specific serving times for each course.
- Tell guests they are now ready to *Cook the Part*.

TUSCAN
farmhouse
DINNER

Tonight you and your guests will create a Tuscan farmhouse experience. Imagine the golden sun setting on rolling hills of grape vines and olive trees, ready for harvest. In the Tuscan spirit, this menu includes simple foods made with fresh, traditional ingredients. ❧ The tablescape can be very simple, with a white tablecloth, a bouquet of flowers from the garden or a small bouquet of sunflowers. If you have brightly colored dishes, tonight is the night to use them. Accent with warm candlelight. ❧ The Grilled Bruschetta with Three Savory Toppings will give your guests a variety of Italian flavors to enjoy while they are cooking. ❧ The Insalata Caprese offers fragrant basil, vine-ripened tomatoes and fresh mozzarella. If tomatoes are not in season, opt for the simple Bibb and Red Leaf Salad. ❧ Cooking Chicken Under a Brick is a technique that creates a crisp, crackling skin and moist, juicy meat. The breasts are pounded to a uniform thickness, marinated with spices and Italian herbs, then grilled while weighted with foil-covered bricks. The chicken is accompanied by white beans spiked with roasted red peppers and ribbons of fresh spinach, and by zucchini that has been treated with a spicy rub before a turn on the grill. ❧ The Fallen Chocolate Cakes are served warm to let you enjoy their fudgy interior.

❧

menu

· · · · · · · ·

APPETIZERS

Grilled Bruschetta with
Three Savory Toppings

Tomato and Basil

Prosciutto and Melon

Eggplant and Roasted Red Pepper

SALAD

Insalata Caprese

or

Bibb and Red Leaf Salad
with Champagne Vinaigrette

ENTRÉE

Chicken Under a Brick

Tuscan White Beans

Grilled Zucchini

DESSERT

Fallen Chocolate Cakes for Eight

· · · · · · · ·

MENU FOR EIGHT

Four Teams of Two
Team A
Team B
Team C
Team D
Total Preparation Time
Before Main Course
2 Hours

grilled bruschetta with three savory toppings

2 large loaves rustic crusty bread or 3 baguettes, cut into ½" thick slices

If using baguettes, cut on the diagonal to create larger slices.

Olive oil for brushing on bread

The appetizer is prepared by the host before guests arrive. Grill the bread 2 hours ahead and prepare the toppings as directed below. Top one-third of the bruschetta with each of the three toppings as guests arrive.

HOST

1. *Grill bread.*

Heat grill to high.

Brush each side of the bread slices with olive oil.

Grill for 1 minute per side or until lightly browned.

Remove to large serving platter.

2. *Serve.*

When ready to serve, top each of the toasted bread slices with 1 of the toppings below.

tomato and basil topping

2 14 ½-ounce cans diced tomatoes, drained

6 cloves garlic, crushed

6 large basil leaves, stems removed, cut into thin ribbons (chiffonade)

2 teaspoons salt

1 teaspoon sugar

½ teaspoon red pepper flakes

½ cup olive oil

Host to prepare the topping early in the day. You will have extra topping. Refrigerate any unused topping. Bring to room temperature before serving. Keeps 1 to 2 weeks.

HOST

1. *Prepare tomato and basil topping.*

Put drained tomatoes into a large empty jar.

Add garlic, basil, salt, sugar and pepper flakes. Mix well.

Pour olive oil over all and allow to rest at room temperature.

MAKES 3 CUPS

prosciutto and melon topping

8   thin slices prosciutto,
    cut in half

½   fresh melon, seeded,
    peeled and thinly sliced

16 mint leaves

Balsamic vinegar

Host to prepare prosciutto and melon 2 hours ahead.

HOST   **1.** *Prepare prosciutto and melon topping.*

Place a piece of the prosciutto on the bread and top with melon and mint. Sprinkle a teaspoon of balsamic vinegar on each piece.

SERVES 8

eggplant and roasted red pepper topping

1   large eggplant

2   red bell peppers

Olive oil for brushing
on vegetables

¼   cup olive oil

1   tablespoon balsamic vinegar

1   teaspoon Dijon mustard

Host to prepare eggplant and roasted red pepper topping 2 hours ahead.

HOST   **1.** *Prepare and grill eggplant.*

Preheat grill to high.

Slice the eggplant crosswise into 1/2" thick slices.

Brush one side of eggplant slices with olive oil and place on grill.

Grill eggplant for 5 minutes; brush the top side of the eggplant with olive oil and turn. Cook for about 3 minutes.

Remove from grill.

Cut the eggplant slices into quarters.

2. *Blacken and prepare peppers.*

Place peppers directly on grill.

Grill until the skin turns black and bubbles up; turn to cook all sides.

Remove from grill and place in a plastic bag for 5 minutes.

Skin the peppers; seed and core them and slice into 1/2" to 1" strips.

3. *Assemble and serve.*

Mix the olive oil, balsamic vinegar and Dijon mustard.

Just before serving, top bread slices with eggplant pieces, adding pepper strips to the top of the eggplant. Put a teaspoon of the olive oil mixture on top of each slice.

SERVES 8

TWO SALAD OPTIONS

. . . .

Two salad options are provided—use Insalata Caprese when beautiful
vine-ripened tomatoes are in season, otherwise use the Bibb and Red Leaf option.

insalata caprese

5   large vine-ripened tomatoes, sliced ⅓" thick or cut into wedges

2   pounds fresh mozzarella (preferably buffalo mozzarella), sliced ⅓" thick

1   bunch fresh basil (about 20 to 30 leaves), stems removed, cut into thin ribbons (chiffonade)

Extra virgin olive oil for drizzling

Coarse salt and pepper to taste

TEAM C   **1. *Prepare salad ingredients.***
Slice tomatoes and place on a large platter. Top each slice with a slice of the mozzarella; top with basil.

TEAM C   **2. *Plate and serve.***
Divide the topped tomato slices among eight individual salad plates at serving time. Drizzle with extra virgin olive oil and season with salt and pepper to taste.

SERVES 8

bibb and red leaf salad with champagne vinaigrette

1   head red leaf lettuce

1   head Bibb lettuce

1   cup dried apricots

1   cup dry roasted almonds (salted)

CHAMPAGNE VINAIGRETTE

¾   cup olive oil

4 ½ tablespoons champagne vinegar

3   tablespoons minced shallot

1 ½ tablespoons country Dijon mustard

1   teaspoon honey

Salt and pepper to taste

HOST   **1. *Prepare lettuces.***
Wash lettuces, spin dry and break large leaves in half. Refrigerate.

TEAM C   **2. *Prepare salad ingredients.***
Coarsely chop dried apricots and almonds.

TEAM B   **3. *Prepare vinaigrette.***
Add ingredients to a jar with a lid and shake vigorously.

TEAM C   **4. *Toss salad, plate and serve.***

SERVES 8

chicken under a brick

8	large chicken breast halves, boneless with skin on
12	garlic cloves, crushed
2	teaspoons dried oregano
1	teaspoon crushed red pepper
2	tablespoons fresh rosemary
2	tablespoons fresh thyme
1½	cups olive oil
2	teaspoons kosher salt
3	tablespoons Gary's Rub* or a purchased grill rub

Canola oil spray for grilling

8 bricks wrapped in foil

Rosemary sprigs or basil leaves for garnish

TEAM A   **1.** *Prepare chicken.*

Wash and dry chicken. Place breasts, one at a time, into a large sealable plastic bag and, using covered bricks, pound to ½" thickness. Remove from bag and repeat with remaining breasts.

TEAM C   **2.** *Make marinade.*

Place garlic, oregano, red pepper, rosemary and thyme in a small food processor and gradually add oil while processing.

TEAM A   **3.** *Marinate chicken.*

Divide the marinade and prepared chicken equally between 2 large sealable plastic bags and turn until chicken is coated.

Refrigerate in marinade until ready to grill.

TEAM A   **4.** *Preheat grill.*

Spray grill rack with canola oil. Preheat grill to medium. Prepare bricks as indicated. Place foil-covered bricks on grill to heat. Be sure to use thick gloves or pot holders to handle heated bricks.

TEAM A   **5.** *Grill and serve.*

Remove chicken from marinade. Sprinkle with salt and Gary's rub.

Place chicken skin side down on grill. Top each breast with a brick and grill until skin is brown and crispy, approximately 5 minutes. Turn chicken and grill until done, another 2 minutes or so. Remove to platter and cover with foil until ready to serve. Garnish with rosemary or basil and serve.

SERVES 8

---

*gary's rub

¼	cup brown sugar
¼	cup sweet paprika
3	tablespoons ground black pepper
1½	tablespoons kosher salt
2	teaspoons garlic powder
2	teaspoons celery seeds
½	teaspoon cayenne pepper
½	teaspoon ground chipotle pepper
1	teaspoon onion powder
½	teaspoon chili powder

Host can prepare weeks ahead.

This rub is used in several recipes throughout this book. We also use it for simple dinners by rubbing chicken, steaks, pork roasts or fish before grilling. It is easy and delicious as it brings out the natural flavors in each of these foods.

HOST   **1.** *Prepare rub.*

Combine ingredients in medium bowl and mix well.
Store in an airtight jar.
Keeps 4-6 months.

cook the Part
GARY

tuscan white beans

3 tablespoons extra virgin olive oil

2 medium onions, chopped

1 12-ounce jar sweet roasted red peppers, drained and chopped

1 head garlic, crushed

5 15-ounce cans cannellini beans, drained and rinsed

1 14-ounce can diced tomatoes, drained

1 ½ teaspoons kosher salt

1 tablespoon fresh rosemary, chopped

1 bay leaf

1 32-ounce box plus 2 cups organic chicken broth

2 cups fresh spinach

TEAM B **1. *Prepare and simmer beans.***

Heat the olive oil in a 6-quart heavy Dutch oven. Sweat the onions for 10 minutes on medium heat. Add the chopped roasted red pepper and the garlic. Heat through.

Add beans, tomatoes, salt, rosemary, bay leaf and 32-ounces chicken broth. Use the remaining 2 cups of broth, as needed, during the cooking process if beans get too dry.

Simmer beans for 1 hour. Turn off heat.

TEAM B **2. *Finish beans and serve.***

Rinse and dry spinach, remove stems and cut into thin ribbons.

Just before serving entrée, reheat beans, add the spinach and simmer for 10 minutes.

SERVES 8 – 12

grilled zucchini

4 large zucchini, washed

Olive oil for brushing zucchini

1 tablespoon Gary's Rub*

*Recipe on page 26.

TEAM C **1. *Prepare zucchini.***

Slice zucchini lengthwise, ½" thick.

Brush with olive oil and sprinkle with Gary's Rub.

TEAM A **2. *Grill zucchini and serve.***

Ensure that grill is heated to medium. Place zucchini directly on grates or use grill racks. Grill until brown; flip over and brown the other side.

SERVES 8

fallen chocolate cakes for eight

8 ounces semisweet chocolate, chopped

8 tablespoons unsalted butter

Butter for ramekins

Approximately ⅔ cup cocoa powder for dusting ramekins and baked cakes, divided

1 vanilla bean

4 large eggs + 1 yolk

¼ teaspoon salt

½ cup sugar

2 tablespoons flour

Whipped cream or ice cream

Raspberries or strawberries for garnish

TEAM D   **1.** *Prepare chocolate.*

Heat chocolate in microwave-safe bowl at 50% power for 2 minutes. Stir and heat for 30 second intervals until chocolate is melted and smooth. Add softened butter and stir until smooth.

TEAM B   **2.** *Prepare ramekins.*

Butter ramekins and sprinkle lightly with cocoa powder. Place on a large baking sheet.

TEAM D   **3.** *Prepare cake batter.*

Cover vanilla bean with hot water for a few minutes to plump. Cut bean in half lengthwise and scrape the inside. Add scrapings to large bowl of electric mixer.

Beat eggs, yolk, vanilla bean scrapings, salt and sugar until smooth, light in color and a thick stream runs from beaters (about 10 minutes).

Add this mixture to the melted chocolate. Gradually add flour. Gently fold until evenly blended.

TEAM D   **4.** *Fill ramekins and chill.*

Divide mixture among 8 prepared ramekins. Refrigerate.

TEAM D   **5.** *Remove ramekins from refrigerator.*

Remove ramekins from refrigerator 1 hour before baking.

TEAM D   **6.** *Bake and serve.*

& TEAM C Preheat oven to 400°. Place baking sheet with ramekins in oven. Bake 12 to 15 minutes until sides are firm, but centers are still soft. Run a sharp knife around the edge of the ramekins to loosen the cakes. Invert cakes onto dessert plates. Dust cakes with cocoa powder. Add whipped cream or ice cream; garnish with raspberries or strawberries and serve.

Note: The fallen chocolate cakes are best served slightly warm. Timing is important. It is best to put the cakes into the oven as the main course is winding down.

SERVES 8

master
PLAN

host preparation

Follow *Host Prep Guidelines* on page 17.

- Determine which salad recipe to include in menu and plan accordingly.

For this menu, follow the **HOST** instructions for the following recipes:

Can be made weeks ahead. . *Gary's Rub*
Early in the day . . . . *Bibb and Red Leaf Salad** (prepare lettuces)
Early in the day . . . . *Tomato and Basil Topping*
2 hours ahead. . . . . *Grilled Bruschetta*
2 hours ahead. . . . . *Prosciutto and Melon Topping*
2 hours ahead. . . . . *Eggplant and Roasted Red Pepper Topping*
As guests arrive. . . . . Top bruschetta with toppings
*If included in menu.

5:30 TO 6:00 PM	GUESTS ARRIVE — HOST PROVIDES GUEST ORIENTATION — PAGE 17			
	TEAM **A**	TEAM **B**	TEAM **C**	TEAM **D**
6:00 TO 7:00 PM	ENJOY APPETIZERS WHILE YOU COOK			
6:00 TO 6:30	• Prepare chicken. • Marinate chicken. (Get marinade from Team C.)	• Prepare and simmer beans. • Prepare ramekins. (Give ramekins to Team D.)	• Prepare marinade for chicken. (Give marinade to Team A.)	• Prepare chocolate for cakes. • Prepare cake batter.
6:30 TO 7:00		• Prepare vinaigrette if serving Bibb and Red Leaf Salad.* (Give vinaigrette to Team C.)*	• Prepare salad ingredients. (Get vinaigrette from Team B.)* • Toss salad.* • Plate and serve.	(Get prepared ramekins from Team B.) • Fill ramekins and chill.
7:00 TO 7:30 PM	ENJOY SALAD			
7:30 TO 8:00	• Preheat grill. • Grill chicken and zucchini. • Serve.	• Finish beans and serve.	• Prepare zucchini. (Give to Team A for grilling.)	• Remove ramekins from refrigerator.
8:00 TO 9:00 PM	ENJOY ENTRÉE			
9:00 TO 9:15			• Prepare whipped cream. (Assist Team D in serving dessert.)	• Bake and serve cakes. (Team C to assist.)
9:15 PM	ENJOY DESSERT			

WORKSTATION:
Counter area
Grill

TOOLS:
Paper towels
Large sealable plastic bags
Foil
8 bricks wrapped in foil
Grilling spatula and tongs

INGREDIENTS:
CHICKEN UNDER A BRICK
8 chicken breast halves,
boneless with skin on
Canola oil spray for grilling
2   teaspoons kosher salt
3   tablespoons Gary's Rub
or a purchased grill rub

5:30 TO 6:00 PM	GUESTS ARRIVE
	Read recipes and Team Plan.
6:00 TO 7:00 PM	ENJOY APPETIZERS WHILE YOU COOK
6:00 TO 6:30	CHICKEN UNDER A BRICK • Prepare chicken. • Marinate chicken. (Get marinade from Team C.)
7:00 TO 8:00 PM	ENJOY SALAD
7:30 TO 8:00	CHICKEN UNDER A BRICK • Preheat grill. • Grill chicken and serve. GRILLED ZUCCHINI (Get zucchini from Team C.) • Grill zucchini and serve.
8:00 TO 9:00 PM	ENJOY ENTRÉE
9:15 PM	ENJOY DESSERT

WORKSTATION:
Counter area
Stovetop

TOOLS:
Chopping board
Knife for chopping
Dutch oven
Garlic press
Can opener
Strainer
Measuring spoons
Measuring cup
8 ramekins
Wax paper
Jar with lid

INGREDIENTS:
TUSCAN WHITE BEANS
3   tablespoons extra virgin olive oil
2   medium onions, chopped
1   12-ounce jar sweet roasted red peppers, drained and chopped
1   head garlic, crushed
5   15-ounce cans cannellini beans, drained and rinsed
1   14-ounce can diced tomatoes, drained
1 ½ teaspoons kosher salt
1   tablespoon fresh rosemary, chopped
1   bay leaf
1   32-ounce box plus 2 cups organic chicken broth
2   cups fresh spinach

FALLEN CHOCOLATE CAKES FOR EIGHT
Butter for ramekins
⅓   cup cocoa powder for dusting ramekins

CHAMPAGNE VINAIGRETTE*
¾   cup olive oil
4 ½ tablespoons champagne vinegar
3   tablespoons minced shallot
1 ½ tablespoons country Dijon mustard
1   teaspoon honey
Salt and pepper to taste
*If serving Bibb and Red Leaf Salad

5:30 TO 6:00 PM	GUESTS ARRIVE
	Read recipes and Team Plan.
6:00 TO 7:00 PM	**ENJOY APPETIZERS WHILE YOU COOK**
6:00 TO 6:30	TUSCAN WHITE BEANS • Prepare and simmer beans. FALLEN CHOCOLATE CAKES FOR EIGHT • Prepare ramekins. (Give ramekins to Team D.)
6:30 TO 7:00	BIBB AND RED LEAF SALAD WITH CHAMPAGNE VINAIGRETTE* • Prepare vinaigrette. (Give vinaigrette to Team C.)
7:00 TO 8:00 PM	**ENJOY SALAD**
7:30 TO 8:00	TUSCAN WHITE BEANS • Finish beans and serve.
8:00 TO 9:00 PM	**ENJOY ENTRÉE**
9:15 PM	**ENJOY DESSERT**

TEAM C

WORKSTATION:
Counter area

TOOLS:
Cutting board
Knife
Food processor
Measuring cup
Measuring spoons
Basting brush
Electric mixer
Bowl
Spoon

INGREDIENTS:
MARINADE FOR
CHICKEN UNDER A BRICK
12 garlic cloves, crushed
2 teaspoon dried oregano
1 teaspoon crushed red pepper
2 tablespoons fresh rosemary
2 tablespoons fresh thyme
1½ cups olive oil

BIBB AND RED LEAF
SALAD WITH
CHAMPAGNE
VINAIGRETTE
Prepared lettuces
1 cup dried apricots
1 cup dry roasted almonds (salted)
OR
INSALATA CAPRESE
5 large vine-ripened tomatoes, sliced ⅓" thick or cut into wedges
2 pounds fresh mozzarella (preferably buffalo mozzarella), sliced ⅓" thick

1 bunch fresh basil (about 20 to 30 leaves), cut into thin ribbons (chiffonade)
Extra virgin olive oil for drizzling
Coarse salt and pepper to taste

GRILLED ZUCCHINI
4 large zucchini, washed
Olive oil for brushing
1 tablespoon Gary's Rub

5:30 TO 6:00 PM	GUESTS ARRIVE		
	Read recipes and Team Plan.		
6:00 TO 7:00 PM	**ENJOY APPETIZERS WHILE YOU COOK**		
6:00 TO 6:30	CHICKEN UNDER A BRICK • Make marinade. (Give marinade to Team A.)		
6:30 TO 7:00	BIBB AND RED SALAD WITH CHAMPAGNE VINAIGRETTE • Prepare salad ingredients. (Get vinaigrette from Team B.) • Toss salad, plate and serve.	Prepare either << OR >>	INSALATA CAPRESE • Prepare salad ingredients. • Plate and serve.
7:00 TO 8:00 PM	**ENJOY SALAD**		
7:30 TO 8:00	GRILLED ZUCCHINI • Prepare zucchini. (Give to Team A for grilling.)		
8:00 TO 9:00 PM	**ENJOY ENTRÉE**		
9:00 TO 9:15	• Prepare whipped cream. (Assist Team D in serving dessert.)		
9:15 PM	**ENJOY DESSERT**		

WORKSTATION:
Counter area
Microwave
Oven

TOOLS:
Chopping board
Knife for chopping
Small microwave-safe bowl
Small knife
Large mixing bowl
Mixer
Rubber spatula
Measuring spoons

Measuring cup
8 ramekins
Baking sheet
Small strainer for dusting
Teaspoon

INGREDIENTS:
FALLEN CHOCLATE
CAKES FOR EIGHT
8   ounces semisweet
    chocolate, chopped
8   tablespoons unsalted
    butter
1   vanilla bean

4   large eggs + 1 yolk
¼   teaspoon salt
½   cup sugar
2   tablespoons flour
⅓   cup cocoa powder for
    dusting baked cakes
Whipped cream or
ice cream
Raspberries or strawberries
for garnish

5:30 TO 6:00 PM	**GUESTS ARRIVE**
	Read recipes and Team Plan.
6:00 TO 7:00 PM	**ENJOY APPETIZERS WHILE YOU COOK**
6:00 TO 6:30	FALLEN CHOCOLATE CAKES FOR EIGHT • Prepare chocolate. • Prepare cake batter.
6:30 TO 7:00	FALLEN CHOCOLATE CAKES FOR EIGHT (Get prepared ramekins from Team B.) • Fill ramekins and chill.
7:00 TO 8:00 PM	**ENJOY SALAD**
7:30 TO 8:00	FALLEN CHOCOLATE CAKES FOR EIGHT • Remove ramekins from refrigerator.
8:00 TO 9:00 PM	**ENJOY ENTRÉE**
9:00 TO 9:15	• Bake and serve. (Team C to assist.)
9:15 PM	**ENJOY DESSERT**

PACIFIC NORTHWEST
seafood
EVENING

This menu evokes thoughts of a brisk autumn breeze off the chilly gray Northwestern Pacific seas. And surprisingly, the meal comes together easily, especially with everyone helping out. ❧ Your guests will want to take the easy maple-ginger salmon recipe home with them to make again in their own kitchens. The fresh salmon entrée is glazed with a sweet-heat mixture of maple syrup, fresh ginger, garlic, chipotle powder and red pepper flakes. ❧ It is accompanied by garlic-sauteed asparagus and buttery mashed sweet potatoes, a nice spin on a comfort food classic. A simple green salad gets a boost in flavor and texture from cherries, walnuts and feta. ❧ Whether you choose to use plums or apples for the streusel cake, it will be a sure hit with its crisp, crumbly topping and tart, tender fruit filling. ❧ The honey cornbread mini muffins will be baked just before guests arrive. Your guests will love catching the aroma of freshly baked cornbread as they walk through the door. A second appetizer, Crab and Red Bell Pepper Crostini, showcases the Pacific Northwest's delicious crab. These will give the guests something to enjoy with their beverage before they "Cook the Part!"

menu

APPETIZERS
Honey Cornbread Mini Muffins

Crab and Red Bell Pepper Crostini

SALAD
Green Salad with Dried Cherries, Walnuts and Feta Cheese

ENTRÉE
Broiled Maple Ginger Salmon

Mashed Sweet Potatoes

Garlic Asparagus

DESSERT
Plum or Apple Streusel Cake

MENU FOR EIGHT
Four Teams of Two
Team A
Team B
Team C
Team D
Total Preparation Time
Before Main Course
2 Hours

honey cornbread mini muffins

1 cup yellow cornmeal
1 cup all-purpose flour
2 teaspoons baking powder
1 teaspoon baking soda
1 teaspoon salt
2 eggs, beaten
¼ cup butter, melted
¾ cup plain yogurt
¾ cup milk
¼ cup honey
1 jalapeño, finely minced
1 cup cooked corn
Butter for mini-muffin pans

Host prepares muffins for guests to enjoy.

Prepare batter and refrigerate for up to 6 hours. Bake muffins approximately 30 to 45 minutes before guests arrive. Serve as an appetizer; any remaining muffins can be served with the main course.

HOST **1.** *Prepare muffin batter.*

Mix together corn meal, flour, baking powder, baking soda and salt in a large bowl. In another bowl, combine eggs, melted butter, yogurt, milk, honey, jalapeño and corn. Add the wet mixture to the dry mixture. Refrigerate until 30 to 45 minutes before baking.

Spoon batter into prepared muffin tins.

HOST **2.** *Bake muffins.*

Preheat oven to 400°. Butter mini muffin pans. Bake muffins for 15 to 20 minutes, or until a toothpick inserted into muffin comes out clean.

MAKES 24 MINI MUFFINS

crab and red bell pepper crostini

1 pound fresh lump crabmeat
½ cup extra virgin olive oil, plus more for brushing on bread
1 roasted red bell pepper, seeded and diced
2 tablespoons green onion, chopped
2 tablespoons lemon juice
½ teaspoon salt
¼ teaspoon freshly ground black pepper
1 baguette

TEAM A **1.** *Preheat oven and prepare crabmeat.*

Preheat oven to 425°.

Pick through crabmeat and remove any shell pieces. Transfer to medium bowl.

TEAM C **2.** *Combine crab mixture.*

Combine crab, olive oil, red bell pepper, green onions, lemon juice, salt and pepper. Mix well.

TEAM B **3.** *Slice bread and bake crostini.*

Slice baguette into ¼" slices. Lay slices on a cookie sheet and brush with olive oil.

Bake for 10 to 12 minutes or until bread is lightly browned.

TEAM D **4.** *Top crostini and serve.*

Top crostini with crab mixture and arrange on serving platter.

SERVES 8 – 10

green salad with dried cherries, walnuts and feta cheese

1   head Romaine lettuce
1   head butter lettuce
1   cup walnuts, toasted
½   cup feta cheese, crumbled
Salt and pepper

SALAD DRESSING
4   tablespoons olive oil
2   tablespoons apple cider vinegar
2   tablespoons minced shallots
1   tablespoon honey
½   cup dried tart cherries

Host to toast walnuts up to 1 week ahead.

TEAM B   **1.** *Wash lettuces.*
Wash lettuces, spin dry and break large leaves in half.

TEAM A   **2.** *Chop walnuts.*
Chop toasted walnuts.

TEAM C   **3.** *Prepare salad dressing.*
Combine salad dressing ingredients in a bowl and whisk.

TEAM A   **4.** *Toss and plate salad.*
Combine lettuce and feta cheese. Add cherry dressing and toss to coat. Sprinkle with toasted walnuts and season with salt and pepper. Plate and serve.

SERVES 8

garlic asparagus

2	pounds asparagus
3	tablespoons olive oil
4	cloves garlic, crushed

TEAM B   **1.** *Preheat oven and prepare asparagus.*

Preheat oven to 425°.

Wash asparagus and trim off hard bottom ends (about 1").

Place asparagus in glass pan.

TEAM B   **2.** *Dress and bake asparagus.*

Pour olive oil over asparagus.

Add garlic to pan and toss asparagus until well coated with garlic and olive oil.

Bake asparagus for 10 to 15 min.

SERVES 8

broiled maple ginger salmon

3/4	cup Grade B maple syrup
1	cup water
4	tablespoons peeled fresh ginger, minced
4	cloves garlic, minced
2	teaspoons dried red pepper flakes
1	teaspoon ground chipotle peppers
8	1" thick pieces salmon fillets (about 6 ounces each)
1	teaspoon salt

Oil for pan

TEAM A **1.** *Prepare maple ginger glaze.*

Combine maple syrup, water and all spices (except salt) in a small saucepan. Simmer over medium heat until mixture is reduced to 1 cup.

TEAM C **2.** *Prepare salmon.*

Rinse fillets and pat dry with paper towels.

Arrange salmon, skin side down, on oiled rack of broiler pan. Season with salt.

TEAM C **3.** *Broil salmon.*

Preheat broiler to medium-high.

Broil salmon about 4" from heat for 7 to 8 minutes until opaque.

Brush salmon with maple ginger glaze and broil until cooked through, approximately 4 to 5 minutes more.

SERVES 8

mashed sweet potatoes

6	large sweet potatoes
6	tablespoons butter
1	tablespoon chopped fresh thyme

Butter for baking dish

TEAM A **1.** *Boil sweet potatoes.*

Boil whole sweet potatoes in large pot until very tender. Drain water.

TEAM A **2.** *Peel and mash sweet potatoes.*

Peel potatoes with a small knife. Place in a large bowl.

Mash with potato masher or large fork.

Add butter and thyme and continue mashing until potatoes are smooth and creamy.

Place in buttered 9" x 13" baking dish and cover with foil until ready to heat and serve.

TEAM A **3.** *Heat and serve sweet potatoes.*

Preheat oven to 350°. Bake potatoes for 15 minutes before serving.

SERVES 8 – 12

plum or apple streusel cake

Butter and flour for cake pan

½ vanilla bean

¼ cup unsalted butter, softened

¾ cup sugar

2 eggs

1 ¾ cup flour

2 teaspoons baking powder

¼ teaspoon salt

¾ cup plain yogurt

Juice of ½ lemon

10 ripe plums
(or 4 Golden Delicious or
Granny Smith apples)

STREUSEL TOPPING

¾ cup flour

¼ cup sugar

6 tablespoons butter, softened

Purchased vanilla ice cream

TEAM D **1.** *Prepare cake pan.*

Butter and flour a 9" x 13" x 2" cake pan.

TEAM D **2.** *Prepare cake batter.*

Cover vanilla bean with hot water for a few minutes to plump.

In large bowl of electric mixer beat butter until creamed, add sugar gradually. Add eggs, one at a time, and beat until light and fluffy.

Cut vanilla bean in half lengthwise and scrape the inside. Add scrapings to batter.

Mix flour, baking powder, and salt in a small bowl.

Add flour mixture and yogurt alternately to creamed butter. Stir in lemon juice. Spread batter in prepared pan.

TEAM C **3.** *Prepare fruit for cake.*

Wash plums, pit and cut into 4 quarters. If using apples, peel, core and quarter. Cut each apple quarter into 4 slices.

TEAM D **4.** *Arrange fruit on top of batter in neat rows.*

TEAM B **5.** *Prepare and add streusel topping to cake.*

Use a fork or pastry cutter to combine flour, sugar and butter until crumbly. Sprinkle over fruit.

TEAM D **6.** *Bake streusel cake.*

Preheat oven to 350˚.

Bake for 40 to 45 minutes until streusel topping is nicely browned.

TEAM D **7.** *Serve streusel cake.*

Cut into serving pieces. Add a scoop of vanilla ice cream to each piece for serving.

SERVES UP TO 18

master PLAN

host preparation

Follow *Host Prep Guidelines* on page 17.

- Selecting quality salmon is key to making this meal special.
- High-quality canned lump crab meat is perfect for the crostini appetizer, but if fresh crab is available, that's even better.
- You can vary the salad ingredients based upon what is in season.

For this menu, follow the **HOST** instructions for the following recipe:

Honey Cornbread Mini Muffins

Up to 6 hours ahead . . . . Prepare muffin batter

30 to 45 minutes ahead . . . . Bake muffins

5:30 TO 6:00 PM	GUESTS ARRIVE — HOST PROVIDES GUEST ORIENTATION — PAGE 17			
	TEAM **A**	TEAM **B**	TEAM **C**	TEAM **D**
6:00 TO 7:30 PM	PREPARE APPETIZERS AND ENJOY WHILE YOU COOK			
6:00 TO 6:30	• Preheat oven and prepare crabmeat.	• Slice bread and bake crostini.	(Get prepared crab from Team A.) • Combine crab mixture. (Give crab mixture to Team D.)	(Get baked crostini from Team B.) (Get crab mixture prepared by Team C.) • Top crostini and serve.
6:30 TO 7:00	• Boil sweet potatoes. • Peel and mash sweet potatoes. • Prepare maple ginger glaze. (Give glaze to Team C.)	• Wash lettuces. (Give lettuces to Team A.)	• Prepare fruit for cake. (Give fruit to Team D.)	• Prepare cake pan. • Prepare cake batter.
7:00 TO 7:30	• Chop walnuts for salad. (Get dressing from Team C and lettuces from Team B.) • Toss and plate salad.	• Prepare and add streusel topping to cake.	• Prepare salad dressing. (Give dressing to Team A.)	(Get fruit from Team C.) • Arrange fruit on top of batter. (Team B to prepare and add streusel topping.) • Bake streusel cake.
7:30 TO 8:00 PM	ENJOY SALAD			
8:00 TO 8:30	• Heat and serve sweet potatoes.	• Preheat oven and prepare asparagus. • Dress and bake asparagus.	• Prepare salmon. • Broil salmon. (Get maple-ginger glaze from Team A.)	
8:30 TO 9:15 PM	ENJOY ENTRÉE			
9:15 TO 9:30		• Ready plates for dessert.		• Serve streusel cake.
9:30 PM	ENJOY DESSERT			

WORKSTATION:
Stovetop
Counter area
Oven

TOOLS:
Medium bowl
Large pot
Knife
Large bowl
Potato masher
9" x 13" glass baking dish
Measuring spoons

Foil
Measuring cup
Small saucepan
Cutting board

INGREDIENTS:
CRAB AND RED BELL PEPPER CROSTINI
1 pound fresh lump crabmeat

MASHED SWEET POTATOES
6 large sweet potatoes
6 tablespoons butter
1 tablespoon chopped fresh thyme
Butter for baking dish

BROILED MAPLE GINGER SALMON
¾ cup grade B maple syrup
1 cup water
4 tablespoons peeled fresh ginger, minced

4 cloves garlic, minced
2 teaspoons dried red pepper flakes
1 teaspoon ground chipotle peppers
1 teaspoon salt

GREEN SALAD
1 cup walnuts, toasted
½ cup feta cheese, crumbled
Salt and pepper

5:30 TO 6:00 PM	**GUESTS ARRIVE**

Read recipes and Team Plan.

6:00 TO 7:30 PM	**PREPARE APPETIZERS AND ENJOY WHILE YOU COOK**

6:00 TO 6:30	CRAB AND RED BELL PEPPER CROSTINI • Preheat oven and prepare crabmeat.
6:30 TO 7:00	MASHED SWEET POTATOES • Boil sweet potatoes. • Peel and mash sweet potatoes. BROILED MAPLE GINGER SALMON • Prepare maple ginger glaze.
7:00 TO 7:30	GREEN SALAD WITH DRIED CHERRIES, WALNUTS AND FETA CHEESE • Chop walnuts. (Get lettuces from Team B.) (Get dressing from Team C.) • Toss and plate salad.

7:30 TO 8:00 PM	**ENJOY SALAD**

8:00 TO 8:30	MASHED SWEET POTATOES • Heat and serve sweet potatoes.

8:30 TO 9:15 PM	**ENJOY ENTRÉE**
9:30 PM	**ENJOY DESSERT**

PACIFIC NORTHWEST SEAFOOD EVENING

WORKSTATION:
Counter area
Oven

TOOLS:
Cutting board
Bread knife
Cookie sheet
Basting brush
Spoon
Salad spinner
Pastry cutter or fork
Small bowl
Knife
Glass pan
Tongs

INGREDIENTS:

CRAB AND RED BELL PEPPER CROSTINI
1 baguette
olive oil to brush on bread

GREEN SALAD
1 head Romaine lettuce
1 head butter lettuce

STREUSEL TOPPING
¾ cup flour
¼ cup sugar
6 tablespoons butter, softened

GARLIC ASPARAGUS
2 pounds asparagus
3 tablespoons olive oil
4 cloves garlic, crushed

5:30 TO 6:00 PM	GUESTS ARRIVE
	Read recipes and Team Plan.
6:00 TO 7:30 PM	**PREPARE APPETIZERS AND ENJOY WHILE YOU COOK**
6:00 TO 6:30	CRAB AND RED BELL PEPPER CROSTINI • Slice bread and bake crostini.
6:30 TO 7:00	GREEN SALAD WITH DRIED CHERRIES, WALNUTS AND FETA CHEESE • Wash lettuces. (Give lettuce to Team A.)
7:00 TO 7:30	PLUM OR APPLE STREUSEL CAKE • Prepare and add streusel topping to cake.
7:30 TO 8:00 PM	ENJOY SALAD
8:00 TO 8:30	GARLIC ASPARAGUS • Preheat oven and prepare asparagus. • Dress and bake asparagus.
8:30 TO 9:15 PM	ENJOY ENTRÉE
9:15 TO 9:30	• Ready plates for dessert.
9:30 PM	ENJOY DESSERT

PACIFIC NORTHWEST SEAFOOD EVENING

WORKSTATION:
Stovetop
Broiler

TOOLS:
Vegetable peeler (if using apples)
Cutting board
Knife
2 Small bowls
Measuring cups
Measuring spoons
Wisk
Paper towels

Rack and broiler pan
Basting brush

INGREDIENTS:
CRAB AND RED BELL PEPPER CROSTINI
½ cup extra virgin olive oil
1 roasted red bell pepper, seeded and diced
2 tablespoons chopped green onion
2 tablespoons lemon juice
½ teaspoon salt
¼ teaspoon freshly ground black pepper

FRUIT FOR PLUM OR APPLE STREUSEL CAKE
10 plums or 4 apples

DRESSING FOR GREEN SALAD
4 tablespoons olive oil
2 tablespoons apple cider vinegar
2 tablespoons minced shallots
1 tablespoon honey
½ cup dried tart cherries

BROILED MAPLE GINGER SALMON
8 1" thick pieces salmon fillet
1 teaspoon salt
Oil for pan

5:30 TO 6:00 PM	GUESTS ARRIVE
	Read recipes and Team Plan.
6:00 TO 7:30 PM	**PREPARE APPETIZERS AND ENJOY WHILE YOU COOK**
6:00 TO 6:30	CRAB AND RED BELL PEPPER CROSTINI (Get prepared crab from Team A.) • Combine crab mixture. (Give crab mixture to Team D.)
6:30 TO 7:00	PLUM OR APPLE STREUSEL CAKE • Prepare fruit for cake. (Give fruit to Team D.)
7:00 TO 7:30	GREEN SALAD WITH DRIED CHERRIES, WALNUTS AND FETA CHEESE • Prepare salad dressing. (Give dressing to Team A.)
7:30 TO 8:00 PM	ENJOY SALAD
8:00 TO 8:30	BROILED MAPLE GINGER SALMON • Prepare salmon. • Broil salmon. (Get maple-ginger glaze from Team A.)
8:30 TO 9:15 PM	ENJOY ENTRÉE
9:30 PM	ENJOY DESSERT

PACIFIC NORTHWEST SEAFOOD EVENING

TEAM D

WORKSTATION:
Counter area
Oven

TOOLS:
Spoon
9" x 13" cake pan
Cup
Mixer
Paring knife
Measuring cups
Measuring spoons
Large mixer bowl

Spatula
Small bowl

INGREDIENTS:
PLUM OR APPLE STREUSEL CAKE
Butter and flour for cake pan
½   vanilla bean
¼   cup unsalted butter
¾   cup sugar
2   eggs
1 ¾ cup flour

2   teaspoons baking powder
¼   teaspoon salt
¾   cup plain yogurt
Juice of ½ lemon

5:30 TO 6:00 PM	GUESTS ARRIVE
	Read recipes and Team Plan.
6:00 TO 7:30 PM	PREPARE APPETIZERS AND ENJOY WHILE YOU COOK
6:00 TO 6:30	CRAB AND RED BELL PEPPER CROSTINI (Get baked crostini from Team B.) (Get crab mixture prepared by Team C.) • Top crostini and serve.
6:30 TO 7:00	PLUM OR APPLE STREUSEL CAKE • Prepare cake pan. • Prepare cake batter.
7:00 TO 7:30	PLUM OR APPLE STREUSEL CAKE (Get fruit from Team C.) • Arrange fruit on top of batter in neat rows. (Team B to prepare and add streusel topping to cake.) • Bake streusel cake.
7:30 TO 8:00 PM	ENJOY SALAD
8:30 TO 9:15 PM	ENJOY ENTRÉE
9:15 TO 9:30	• Serve streusel cake.
9:30 PM	ENJOY DESSERT

comfort
FOOD

Comfort foods are simple classics that provide emotional satisfaction. They have a timeless quality that draws us back to them every few years, so they never really go out of style. The host will greet guests with appetizers prepared ahead of time: a shrimp cocktail with homemade spicy cocktail sauce and a platter of purchased pâté, cornichons and crusty breads or crackers. A green salad gets a flavor boost with white peaches, goat cheese and candied almonds. The beef short ribs are braised to tender perfection, and the resulting sumptuous red wine reduction sauce makes a heavenly accompaniment to the roasted garlic mashed potatoes. Steamed baby carrots complete the entrée, which stands up to a good Cabernet Sauvignon. The Apple Tarte Tatin dessert is a special addition to this menu, and must be prepared in an iron skillet to be authentic. Sliced apples are artfully arranged in layers in the pan and caramelized on the stovetop. The pan is topped with flaky pastry dough, baked until golden brown, and then flipped upside down onto a serving dish. Vanilla ice cream sets it off nicely. You may consider serving a small cognac at the end of this meal to add a bit of the "supper club" feel to the experience.

menu

APPETIZERS

Classic Shrimp Cocktail
Spicy Cocktail Sauce

Pâté, Cornichons,
Artisanal Crackers and Crusty Bread

SALAD

Mixed Greens with White Peaches,
Goat Cheese and Candied Almonds

ENTRÉE

Braised Beef Short Ribs with
Veal Demi-Glace and
Wine Reduction Sauce

Roasted Garlic Mashed Potatoes

Steamed Baby Carrots

DESSERT

Apple Tarte Tatin

Vanilla Ice Cream

MENU FOR EIGHT

Four Teams of Two
Team A
Team B
Team C
Team D
Total Preparation Time
Before Main Course
2 ½ Hours

Comfort Food
Hosted by Paul and Jennifer Cayer
Saturday, June 4, 2011

Appetizer
Classic Shrimp Cocktail
Spicy Cocktail Sauce
Paté with Cornichons
Artisanal Crackers and Crusty Bread

Salad
Mixed Greens with Yellow Peaches, Goat
Cheese and Candied Almonds

Main Course
Braised Beef Short Ribs with Veal Demi-
Glace and Wine Reduction Sauce
Roasted Garlic Mashed Potatoes
Sauteed Baby Carrots

Dessert
Apple Tarte Tatin
Vanilla Ice Cream

Host prepares appetizers before guests arrive. The cocktail sauce can be prepared up to 2 days ahead.
The shrimp should be cooked and chilled early in the day. The pâté platter can be prepared up to 1 hour ahead.

classic shrimp cocktail

24	large shrimp (16 to 20 count per pound), peeled and deveined, tails on	
1	lemon, quartered	
2	teaspoons salt	

HOST

1. *Cook shrimp.*

Bring a large pot of water to a boil with lemon and salt.

Add shrimp to boiling water and return to boil. Cook for approximately 3 minutes until shrimp are pink and opaque. Remove from water and plunge into ice water. Drain and chill until ready to serve.

This recipe provides for 3 large shrimp per guest.

SERVES 8

spicy cocktail sauce

1	cup catsup
2	tablespoons fresh lemon juice
6	drops Tabasco sauce
1	teaspoon Worcestershire sauce
2	tablespoons chili sauce
2	tablespoons horseradish
1	tablespoon grated onion
½	teaspoon salt
1	tablespoon minced parsley

HOST

1. *Prepare cocktail sauce.*

Combine all ingredients in a small bowl. Serve the shrimp on lettuce leaves surrounding the cocktail sauce, or prepare individual servings of sauce with shrimp around the edges of a small cocktail bowl.

MAKES 1 ½ CUPS

pâté, cornichons, artisanal crackers and crusty bread

HOST

1. *Arrange pâté platter.*

Purchase a ½" slice of high-quality pâté at a cheese shop or deli.

Serve with the cornichons, artisanal crackers and crusty bread.

mixed greens with white peaches, goat cheese and candied almonds

1	large head butter lettuce, washed and dried
1	large head red leaf lettuce, washed and dried
4	ripe white peaches
1	cup candied almonds
8	ounces goat cheese, cut into small cubes

SALAD DRESSING

⅓	cup olive oil
2	tablespoons red wine vinegar
2	tablespoons honey Dijon mustard

Salt and pepper to taste

CANDIED ALMONDS

1	cup sliced almonds
1	tablespoon butter
1	tablespoon honey

HOST **1.** *Prepare candied almonds.*

Melt butter in a skillet and add almonds. Sauté until almonds are coated and begin to brown. Add honey and mix into almonds, stirring for a few minutes. Remove from the heat. Cool; store in a closed container for up to 1 week.

TEAM A **2.** *Prepare salad ingredients.*

Cut peaches into halves, remove pit and cut each half into six thin slices.

TEAM C **3.** *Make salad dressing.*

Mix dressing ingredients in a small jar with a lid and shake until well combined.

TEAM A **4.** *Toss salad, plate and serve.*

Toss the lettuces with dressing.

Divide among individual salad plates and attractively arrange peaches across lettuces. Top with the candied almonds and goat cheese.

SERVES 8

Note: Change fruit based on seasonal availability. A nice adaption is pears, Gorgonzola cheese and caramelized walnuts.

braised beef short ribs with veal demi-glace and wine reduction sauce

WINE REDUCTION SAUCE

2	bottles red wine (such as a cabernet sauvignon or merlot)
½	cup veal demi-glace concentrate (purchased)
4	cups water
2	teaspoons fresh thyme
1	bay leaf
6	tablespoons country Dijon mustard

8	pounds beef short ribs, bones removed*
1	teaspoon fine sea salt
1	teaspoon black pepper
6	tablespoons canola oil, divided
2	onions, finely chopped
6	carrots, finely chopped
6	garlic cloves, minced or crushed
1	pound crimini mushrooms, washed, trimmed and quartered

* Ask butcher to remove bones

1. *Prepare wine reduction sauce.*

HOST Pour wine into a large saucepan. Simmer until reduced by half (approximately 40 minutes).

TEAM A Add the veal demi-glace, water, thyme, bay leaf and mustard to the wine reduction sauce. Stir to mix well.

Reduce further by simmering for an additional 15 minutes.

TEAM B **2.** *Brown ribs and vegetables.*

Wash ribs and pat dry with paper towels; sprinkle with salt and pepper. Heat 2 tablespoons canola oil in each of 2 large (4-to 5-quart) sauté pans with lids. Sauté ribs on all sides until nicely browned (about 8 to 10 minutes). Remove ribs to plates.

Add another tablespoon of oil to each pan and scrape up browned bits of meat. Divide the following vegetables equally between both pans: Add onions and sauté for about 5 minutes until golden; add carrots and sauté for 3 minutes; add garlic and sauté for 1 additional minute.

TEAM B **3.** *Braise ribs.*

Add the wine reduction sauce to the vegetables, dividing it equally between the 2 pans. Divide the browned ribs equally between the 2 pans, cover and simmer for 1½ hours until meat is very tender, stirring occasionally and adding a bit of water if necessary. Add the mushrooms for the last 20 minutes of braising.

SERVES 8

roasted garlic mashed potatoes

2	heads garlic for garlic paste
4	tablespoons olive oil, divided
4	pounds Yukon gold potatoes
2	teaspoons salt
4	tablespoons butter
1	cup milk, vegetable broth or chicken broth

TEAM C   **1. *Prepare and bake garlic for mashed potatoes.***

Heat oven to 375°. Cut off the top quarter (pointy side) of the heads of garlic.

Drizzle with 2 tablespoons olive oil, wrap in foil and place in a loaf pan.

Bake for 50 minutes. Cool.

TEAM C   **2. *Prepare garlic paste.***

Remove cloves from skins by picking them out with a sharp pointed knife.

Smash cloves with a fork until a smooth paste is formed.

Mix garlic with the remaining 2 tablespoons of olive oil. Reserve the garlic paste for mixing into the mashed potatoes later.

TEAM B   **3. *Prepare potatoes.***

Peel potatoes, cut into quarters and cover with cold water in large stock pot.

TEAM B   **4. *Boil potatoes.***

Add salt to potatoes.

Boil potatoes for approximately 30 minutes.

Test for doneness and drain.

TEAM A   **5. *Mash and finish potatoes.***

Mash potatoes. Stir in garlic paste and butter.

Heat the desired liquid and add to the potatoes.

Mash until smooth.

Cover and keep warm until ready to serve.

SERVES 8 - 10

steamed baby carrots

24	whole baby carrots with some green tops, scrubbed, not peeled

TEAM C   **1. *Prepare steamed baby carrots.***

Place water in a steamer pot and bring to boil.

Put prepared carrots in steamer basket.

Steam for 6 to 8 minutes until desired tenderness.

SERVES 8

apple tarte tatin

CRUST

1 ¾	cup flour
1	teaspoon salt
9	tablespoons cold unsalted butter

4 to 5 tablespoons ice water

12	large Granny Smith apples (6 pounds)

Zest and juice of one lemon

2	cups sugar, divided
9	tablespoons unsalted butter

Vanilla ice cream

TEAM C   **1.** *Preheat oven and prepare crust.*

Preheat oven to 425°. Use a food processor to mix flour, salt and butter until crumbs are formed. Add ice water and pulse until mixture holds together nicely. Wrap dough in wax paper and chill until needed.

TEAM D   **2.** *Prepare apples.*

Peel, core and quarter apples. Slice each quarter into 3 slices. Add the lemon zest and juice to the apples. Add ¾ cup of the sugar and stir. Let steep for 20 to 30 minutes then drain the apples.

TEAM D   **3.** *Make caramel and cook apples.*

Use a 12" iron skillet to melt butter. Add the remaining 1¼ cups sugar. Stir until a brown, bubbly caramel forms.

Add the apples to the caramel, arranging them in a nice pattern around the pan. Continue to add apples in subsequent layers, filling in the empty spaces until all apples have been added. Cook about 15 minutes, covered; baste the apples with a bulb baster periodically. When the syrup is nicely thickened, remove the pan from heat.

TEAM D   **4.** *Prepare and bake Tarte Tatin.*

Roll the dough out into a 13" circle on parchment paper. Center the dough over the apples, forming an edge with the excess dough. Bake 20 minutes in a preheated oven until the crust is nicely browned. Remove from the oven and tilt pan to ensure that juices are not too thin. If necessary, cook down juices on the stovetop until juices are thick.

TEAM D   **5.** *Flip Tarte Tatin.*

Place a large heat-resistant serving platter over the skillet. Flip the pan upside down onto the serving platter. You may need help with this as the pan is red hot and very heavy.

TEAM C
& TEAM D   **6.** *Serve dessert.*

Cut Tarte Tatin into slices.

Serve with vanilla ice cream.

SERVES 12

master **PLAN**

host preparation

Follow *Host Prep Guidelines* on page 17.

For this menu, follow the **HOST** instructions for the following recipes:

Early in the day . . . . . *Mixed Greens* (candied almonds)

Early in the day . . . . . *Classic Shrimp Cocktail and Spicy Cocktail Sauce*

Up to 1 hour ahead . . . *Pâté, Cornichons, Artisanal Crackers and Crusty Bread*

1 hour ahead. . . . . . . *Braised Beef Short Ribs* (reduction sauce)

5:30 TO 6:00 PM	GUESTS ARRIVE – HOST PROVIDES GUEST ORIENTATION – PAGE 17

	TEAM A	TEAM B	TEAM C	TEAM D
6:00 TO 7:30 PM	**PREPARE APPETIZERS AND ENJOY WHILE YOU COOK**			
6:00 TO 7:00	• Prepare wine reduction sauce. • Prepare salad ingredients.	• Brown ribs and vegetables. • Braise ribs.	• Preheat oven and prepare crust for Tarte Tatin. • Prepare and bake garlic for mashed potatoes. • Prepare garlic paste.	• Prepare apples for Tarte Tatin. • Make caramel and cook apples.
7:00 TO 7:30	(Get salad dressing from Team C.) • Toss salad, plate and serve.	• Prepare potatoes. • Boil potatoes.	• Make salad dressing. (Give dressing to Team A.)	• Prepare and bake Tarte Tatin. (Team C prepared crust.)
7:30 TO 8:00 PM	**ENJOY SALAD**			
8:00 TO 8:30	(Get boiled potatoes from Team B.) (Get garlic paste from Team C.) Mash and finish potatoes.	• Serve ribs.	• Prepare steamed baby carrots.	• Flip Tarte Tatin.
8:30 TO 9:30 PM	**ENJOY ENTRÉE**			
9:30 TO 9:45			(Assist Team D in serving dessert.)	• Serve Tarte Tatin with vanilla ice cream. (Team C to assist.)
9:45 PM	**ENJOY DESSERT**			

WORKSTATION:
Counter area
Sink
Stovetop

TOOLS:
Measuring cups
Measuring spoons
Cutting board
Knife
Potato masher
Small saucepan

INGREDIENTS:

WINE REDUCTION SAUCE
Reduced red wine
½ cup veal demi-glace concentrate (purchased)
4 cups water
2 teaspoons fresh thyme
1 bay leaf
6 tablespoons country Dijon mustard

MIXED GREENS WITH WHITE PEACHES, GOAT CHEESE AND CANDIED ALMONDS
Prepared lettuces
4 ripe white peaches
1 cup candied almonds
1 cup goat cheese, cut into small cubes

ROASTED GARLIC MASHED POTATOES
4 tablespoons butter
1 cup milk, vegetable broth or chicken broth

5:30 TO 6:00 PM	**GUESTS ARRIVE**
	Read recipes and Team Plan.
6:00 TO 7:30 PM	**ENJOY APPETIZERS WHILE YOU COOK**
6:00 TO 7:00	BRAISED BEEF SHORT RIBS WITH VEAL DEMI-GLACE AND WINE REDUCTION SAUCE • Prepare wine reduction sauce. (Host has started the wine reduction sauce.)
7:00 TO 7:30	MIXED GREENS WITH WHITE PEACHES, GOAT CHEESE AND CANDIED ALMONDS • Prepare salad ingredients. (Get salad dressing from Team C.) • Toss salad, plate and serve.
7:30 TO 8:00 PM	**ENJOY SALAD**
8:00 TO 8:30	ROASTED GARLIC MASHED POTATOES (Get boiled potatoes from Team B.) (Get garlic paste from Team C.) • Mash and finish potatoes.
8:30 TO 9:30 PM	**ENJOY ENTRÉE**
9:45 PM	**ENJOY DESSERT**

COMFORT FOOD

WORKSTATION:
Stovetop

TOOLS:
Paper towels
2 large (4-to 5-quart) sauté pans with lids
2 large plates
Wooden spoon
Potato peeler
Large stock pot

INGREDIENTS:
BRAISED BEEF
SHORT RIBS WITH VEAL
DEMI-GLACE AND WINE
REDUCTION SAUCE
8 pounds beef short ribs
1 teaspoon fine sea salt
1 teaspoon black pepper
6 tablespoons canola oil, divided
2 onions, finely chopped
6 carrots, finely chopped
6 garlic cloves, minced or crushed
1 pound crimini mushrooms, washed, trimmed and quartered

ROASTED GARLIC
MASHED POTATOES
4 pounds Yukon gold potatoes
2 teaspoons salt

5:30 TO 6:00 PM	GUESTS ARRIVE
	Read recipes and Team Plan.
6:00 TO 7:30 PM	ENJOY APPETIZERS WHILE YOU COOK
6:00 TO 7:00	BRAISED BEEF SHORT RIBS WITH VEAL DEMI-GLACE AND WINE REDUCTION SAUCE • Brown ribs and vegetables. • Braise ribs.
7:00 TO 7:30	ROASTED GARLIC MASHED POTATOES • Prepare potatoes. • Boil potatoes.
7:30 TO 8:00 PM	ENJOY SALAD
8:00 TO 8:30	BRAISED BEEF SHORT RIBS WITH VEAL DEMI-GLACE AND WINE REDUCTION SAUCE • Serve ribs.
8:30 TO 9:30 PM	ENJOY ENTRÉE
9:45 PM	ENJOY DESSERT

WORKSTATION:
Counter area
Oven

TOOLS:
Food processor
Measuring cups
Measuring spoons
Wax paper
Knife
Foil
Loaf pan for garlic
Small knife
Fork

Small bowl
Jar with lid
Steamer Pot

INGREDIENTS:
CRUST FOR
APPLE TARTE TATIN
1 ¾   cups flour
1   teaspoon salt
9   tablespoons cold
    unsalted butter
4 to 5 tablespoons
    ice water

GARLIC PASTE FOR
ROASTED GARLIC
MASHED POTATOES
2   heads garlic for garlic
    paste
4   tablespoons olive oil,
    divided

SALAD DRESSING
⅓   cup olive oil
2   tablespoons red wine
    vinegar
2   tablespoons honey
    Dijon mustard
Salt and pepper to taste

STEAMED BABY
CARROTS
24   baby carrots, scrubbed

5:30 TO 6:00 PM	**GUESTS ARRIVE**
	Read recipes and Team Plan.
6:00 TO 7:30 PM	**ENJOY APPETIZERS WHILE YOU COOK**
6:00 TO 7:00	APPLE TARTE TATIN • Preheat oven and prepare crust. ROASTED GARLIC MASHED POTATOES • Prepare and bake garlic for mashed potatoes. • Prepare garlic paste. (Give to Team A.)
7:00 TO 7:30	MIXED GREENS WITH WHITE PEACHES, GOAT CHEESE AND CANDIED ALMONDS • Make Salad Dressing. (Give dressing to Team A.)
7:30 TO 8:00 PM	**ENJOY SALAD**
8:00 TO 8:30	STEAMED BABY CARROTS • Prepare steamed baby carrots.
8:30 TO 9:30 PM	**ENJOY ENTRÉE**
9:30 TO 9:45	APPLE TARTE TATIN (Assist Team D in serving dessert.)
9:45 PM	**ENJOY DESSERT**

COMFORT FOOD

TEAM D

WORKSTATION:
Counter area
Oven

TOOLS:
Apple peeler
Knife
Cutting board
Measuring cups
Measuring spoons
Large bowl
12" Iron skillet
Bulb baster
Rolling pin
Parchment paper
Large knife

INGREDIENTS:
APPLE TARTE TATIN
12 large Granny Smith
  apples (6 pounds)
Zest and juice of one lemon
2 cups sugar, divided
9 tablespoons unsalted
  butter
Vanilla ice cream

5:30 TO 6:00 PM	GUESTS ARRIVE
	Read recipes and Team Plan.
6:00 TO 7:30 PM	ENJOY APPETIZERS WHILE YOU COOK
6:00 TO 7:00	APPLE TARTE TATIN • Prepare apples. • Make caramel and cook apples.
7:00 TO 7:30	• Prepare and bake Tarte Tatin.
7:30 TO 8:00 PM	ENJOY SALAD
8:00 TO 8:30	• Flip Tarte Tatin.
8:30 TO 9:30 PM	ENJOY ENTRÉE
9:30 TO 9:45	• Serve dessert. (Team C to assist.)
9:45 PM	ENJOY DESSERT

A TASTE OF
baja

The bold, beach-style flavors of the Baja Peninsula will have your guests thinking sun, surf and sandals. Set the mood with Margaritas in colorful glasses or with Mexican beer. Guests make the guacamole and salsas for the appetizers, but they come together quickly because the host will chop all the ingredients ahead of time. These are not your ordinary chip dips. The Citrus Guacamole gets its bright flavor notes from orange and lime juices. The Tomatillo Salsa packs some heat from serrano chiles. Vine-ripened tomatoes play the starring role in the Pico de Gallo. Baja fish tacos are fresh and festive, with a casual feel. The spice-rubbed grilled halibut offers a lighter, more flavorful version than heavy batter-fried fish. Instead of serving them with the usual white cabbage, we chose red cabbage for added color. Accompaniments include Mexican Rice and Black Beans with Queso Añejo, a firm, aged Mexican cheese. The guacamole and salsas make a repeat performance as taco toppings. Serve everything buffet-style, so guests can customize their tacos to suit their tastes. For dessert, cool creamy vanilla ice cream offsets the spicy kick in the Chocolate Chipotle Brownie Cake.

menu

APPETIZERS

Citrus Guacamole

Pico de Gallo

Tomatillo Salsa

Yellow and Blue Corn Chips

SALAD

Baja Salad

ENTRÉE

*Fish Tacos with Shredded
Red Cabbage
and White Sauce*

Corn Tortillas

Mexican Rice

Black Beans with Queso Añejo

DESSERT

Chocolate Chipotle Brownie Cake

Vanilla Ice Cream

Espresso (optional)

MENU FOR EIGHT

Four Teams of Two
Team A
Team B
Team C
Team D
Total Preparation Time
Before Main Course
2 Hours

citrus guacamole

6	large, ripe avocados	
3	tablespoons cilantro leaves	
½	small red onion, chopped	
3	cloves garlic, crushed	
1	jalapeño, minced	
½	orange	
½	lime	
1	teaspoon salt	

TEAM C   **1.** *Prepare ingredients.*

Peel, pit and mash avocados with a fork or work with two large spoons to break them down by cutting across them. Chop cilantro.

TEAM C   **2.** *Mix and serve.*

Squeeze orange and lime juice over avocados. Add remaining ingredients and mix.

Serve with assorted corn chips.

Serve remainder with fish tacos.

MAKES 2 CUPS

pico de gallo

6	large ripe red tomatoes	
½	cup cilantro leaves	
1	white onion, finely chopped	
2	jalapeños, minced	
1	lime	
Sea salt		

TEAM B   **1.** *Prepare vegetables.*

Chop tomatoes. Chop cilantro. Squeeze juice from lime.

TEAM B   **2.** *Mix and serve.*

Combine all ingredients in bowl.

Add salt to taste.

Serve with assorted corn chips.

MAKES 2 CUPS

tomatillo salsa

6	tomatillos
½	cup white onion, chopped
3	garlic cloves, crushed
1	Serrano chili, stemmed and minced
¼	cup fresh cilantro leaves
½	teaspoon sea salt
2	tablespoons lime juice

TEAM B   **1.** *Prepare vegetables.*

Husk and wash the tomatillos and cut into quarters.

TEAM B   **2.** *Process.*

Use food processor to pulse the tomatillos until chopped; add the onion, garlic, Serrano chili, cilantro and salt.

Add lime juice.

Process until smooth.

TEAM B   **3.** *Mix and serve.*

Transfer to a serving bowl.

Serve with assorted corn chips.

MAKES 1 ½ CUPS

baja salad

2   heads Bibb lettuce

1   cup arugula

2   ripe avocados

1   ripe mango or orange

½   red onion, thinly sliced

½   cup raw shelled pumpkin
    seeds, toasted with
    ½ teaspoon dry grill rub*

¾   cup queso añejo
    (can substitute feta)

Salt and pepper to taste

* Purchase a spice rub or make
Gary's Rub – recipe on page 26.

SALAD DRESSING

¼   cup fresh cilantro leaves

3   garlic cloves, crushed

⅓   cup lime juice, squeezed fresh

¾   cup olive oil

2   teaspoons honey

½   jalapeño, minced

TEAM A **1.** *Prepare salad ingredients.*

Wash lettuces and arugula, spin dry and break large leaves in half.

Peel avocados and mango. Chop into ½" pieces.

TEAM B **2.** *Prepare salad dressing.*

Chop cilantro.

Combine garlic, lime juice, cilantro, olive oil, honey and jalapeño in small jar.

Shake vigorously.

TEAM A **3.** *Toss salad and plate.*

Mix lettuce, arugula, avocado, mango or orange, red onion and pumpkin seeds.

Toss with salad dressing.

Place on plates or in salad bowls and sprinkle with queso añejo.

Add salt and pepper to taste.

SERVES 8

fish tacos with shredded red cabbage and white sauce

3 pounds fresh halibut (1" thick)

3 tablespoons dry grill rub*

Canola oil spray

½ head red cabbage

4 limes

16 Corn tortillas

WHITE SAUCE FOR FISH TACOS

½ cup plain yogurt

½ cup mayonnaise

1 lime

½ jalapeño, minced

1 teaspoon capers, minced

½ teaspoon ground cumin

1 teaspoon dry grill rub*

* Purchase a spice rub or make Gary's Rub – recipe on page 26.

TEAM B   1. *Prepare fish.*

Preheat grill to medium-high heat. Wash fish and pat dry. Sprinkle with rub. Spray with canola oil.

TEAM A   2. *Prepare white sauce.*

Mix yogurt, mayonnaise, juice of 1 lime, jalapeño, capers, cumin and rub in a small mixing bowl.

TEAM A   3. *Shred cabbage.*

Use a sharp knife to cut cabbage in half and remove the core (heart). Shred each of the cabbage halves.

TEAM B   4. *Grill and serve.*

Grill the fish for 7 minutes on the first side and then flip and grill for 4 minutes more and remove. Let rest for 5 minutes.

Place fish on large platter surrounded by shredded cabbage and lime wedges. Serve white sauce in a separate bowl.

TEAM A   5. *Cut limes.*

Cut limes into wedges for the fish taco serving platter.

TEAM C   6. *Heat tortillas.*

Heat tortillas on the grill before serving.

Wrap in attractive kitchen towel for serving.

SERVES 8

mexican rice

2	tablespoons olive oil
½	yellow onion, chopped
3	cloves garlic, crushed
2	cups long grain rice
1	32-ounce box organic chicken broth
2	teaspoons salt
1	12-ounce jar roasted red peppers, chopped
2	tablespoons parsley, chopped

TEAM C **1.** *Sauté vegetables.*

Heat olive oil in 2-quart saucepan over medium heat.

Sauté onion in the olive oil until translucent. Add garlic and sauté for 1 minute. Add the rice and stir until all grains are coated with oil and turn golden.

TEAM C **2.** *Cook rice.*

Add broth and salt, cover and simmer for 20 minutes. Add the peppers and parsley. Cook another 5 minutes or until rice is tender.

SERVES 8

black beans with queso añejo

2	15-ounce cans black beans
1	tablespoon olive oil
1	white or yellow onion, finely chopped
4	garlic cloves, crushed
½	teaspoon ground cumin
1	14 ½-ounce can organic chicken broth
Salt and pepper to taste	
½	cup queso añejo

TEAM D **1.** *Drain black beans.*

TEAM D **2.** *Cook beans.*

Heat oil in 2-quart saucepan over medium-high heat.

Add onion and sauté until translucent; add garlic and sauté 1 minute.

Add cumin, drained beans and ½ of broth and cook 5 minutes, stirring occasionally.

Coarsely mash beans with potato masher. Add the remainder of the broth.

Boil until thick, stirring frequently, about 20 minutes.

TEAM D **3.** *Season beans and serve.*

Season to taste with salt and pepper. Transfer to serving bowl.

Sprinkle with queso añejo and serve.

SERVES 8

chocolate chipotle brownie cake

Butter and flour for cake pan

¾ cup butter

6 ounces semi-sweet chocolate, chips or pieces

4 ounces unsweetened chocolate, chips or pieces

4 large eggs

¾ cup sugar

½ cup brown sugar

2 teaspoons vanilla extract

1 ½ teaspoons chipotle powder

¼ teaspoon cayenne pepper

1 teaspoon cinnamon

1 cup all-purpose flour

½ cup raisins, soaked overnight in beer, drained

½ cup hazelnuts, chopped and toasted

Powdered sugar for garnish

Vanilla ice cream, if desired

Espresso shots (optional)

TEAM D **1.** *Prepare cake pan and preheat oven.*

Preheat oven to 350°.

Butter and flour a 10" springform pan or 9" square pan.

TEAM D **2.** *Prepare cake batter.*

Put the butter and chocolate in a microwaveable dish and melt them together on HIGH for a few seconds at a time until the chocolate is melted. Stir well and cool.

Place the eggs in the bowl of electric mixer and beat until they start to thicken. Add the sugars. Continue beating until the mixture is light and fluffy. Stir in vanilla and chocolate mixture.

TEAM D **3.** *Combine ingredients for cake.*

Combine and sift the chipotle powder, cayenne pepper, cinnamon and flour.

Gently stir the combined dry ingredients into the wet ingredients. Gently add the raisins and hazelnuts, stirring until just combined. Don't over-mix.

TEAM D **4.** *Bake cake.*

Pour the cake mixture into the greased and floured springform pan. Bake until set, 25 to 30 minutes. Cool in the pan. Invert onto a serving dish, dust with powdered sugar and cut into wedges.

TEAM C **5.** *Serve cake.*
& TEAM D Serve cake, adding a scoop of vanilla ice cream, and top with a shot of espresso, if desired.

master PLAN

host preparation

Follow *Host Prep Guidelines* on page 17.

- Toast pumpkin seeds with grill rub for salad.
- Soak the raisins overnight for the Chocolate Chipotle Brownie Cake.
- The following chopping grid is provided to assist in preparing your work stations. After chopping each of the ingredients

in the table below, put them in prep bowls with a label (can use Postit notes or index cards) indicating the contents, the recipe and the appropriate team. (i.e., ½ cup chopped white onion, Tomatillo Salsa, Team B.)

- Put out assorted blue and yellow corn chips for salsas and guacamole, using colorful bowls or baskets lined with colorful napkins.

	TOMATILLO SALSA	PICO DE GALLO	GUACAMOLE	BAJA SALAD	MEXICAN RICE	BLACK BEANS	WHITE SAUCE
onions, chopped	½ c. white	1 white	½ small red		½ yellow	1 white or yellow	
garlic, crushed	3 cloves		3 cloves	3 cloves	3 cloves	4 cloves	
jalapeño, minced		2	2	½			½
Serrano, minced	1						
GIVE TO >>	Team B	Team B	Team C	Team B	Team C	Team C	Team A

5:30 TO 6:00 PM	GUESTS ARRIVE — HOST PROVIDES GUEST ORIENTATION — PAGE 17

	TEAM A	TEAM B	TEAM C	TEAM D
6:00 TO 7:00 PM	**PREPARE APPETIZERS AND ENJOY WHILE YOU COOK**			
6:00 TO 6:30	• Prepare salad ingredients. • Prepare white sauce for fish tacos.	• Prepare Pico de Gallo. • Prepare Tomatillo Salsa. • Mix and serve salsas.	• Prepare ingredients for guacamole. • Mix and serve guacamole.	• Prepare cake pan and preheat oven. • Prepare cake batter.
6:30 TO 7:00	• Shred cabbage for fish tacos. • Toss salad and plate.	• Prepare salad dressing.	• Sauté vegetables for rice.	• Combine ingredients for cake.
7:00 TO 7:30 PM	**ENJOY SALAD**			
7:30 TO 8:00	• Cut limes into wedges for fish serving platter.	• Prepare fish. • Grill and serve fish.	• Cook rice. • Heat tortillas.	• Drain black beans. • Cook beans. • Season beans and serve. • Bake cake.
8:00 TO 9:00 PM	**ENJOY ENTRÉE**			
9:00 TO 9:15			• Serve cake. (Team D to assist.)	• Serve cake. (Team C to assist.)
9:15 PM	**ENJOY DESSERT**			

WORKSTATION:
Counter area

TOOLS:
Salad spinner
Knives
Cutting board
Juicer
Measuring cups
Measuring spoons
Spoon
Small mixing bowl

INGREDIENTS:
BAJA SALAD
2   heads Bibb lettuce
1   cup arugula
2   ripe avocados
1   ripe mango or orange
½   cup red onion,
    thinly sliced
½   cup pumpkin seeds,
    toasted
¾   cup queso añejo
Salt and pepper

WHITE SAUCE FOR
FISH TACOS
½   cup plain yogurt
½   cup mayonnaise
1   lime
½   jalepeno, minced
1   teaspoon capers,
    minced
½   teaspoon ground cumin
1   teaspoon Gary's Rub

FISH TACOS
½   head red cabbage
4   limes

5:30 TO 6:00 PM	GUESTS ARRIVE
	Read recipes and Team Plan.
6:00 TO 7:00 PM	**PREPARE APPETIZERS AND ENJOY WHILE YOU COOK**
6:00 TO 6:30	BAJA SALAD • Prepare salad ingredients. FISH TACOS • Prepare white sauce • Shred cabbage.
6:30 TO 7:00	BAJA SALAD • Toss salad and plate.
7:00 TO 7:30 PM	ENJOY SALAD
7:30 TO 8:00	FISH TACOS • Cut limes into wedges for serving platter.
8:00 TO 9:00 PM	ENJOY ENTRÉE
9:15 PM	ENJOY DESSERT

A TASTE OF BAJA

WORKSTATION:
Counter area
Grill

TOOLS:
Knife
Cutting board
Food processor
Measuring spoons
Juicer
Mixing spoons
Jar
Paper towels
Spatula for grilling
Grill rack (optional)

INGREDIENTS:

PICO DE GALLO
6   large ripe red tomatoes
½   cup cilantro leaves
1   white onion, finely chopped
2   jalpeños, minced
1   lime
Sea salt

TOMATILLO SALSA
6   tomatillos
½   cup white onion, chopped
3   garlic cloves, crushed

1   Serrano chili, stemmed and minced
¼   cup fresh cilantro leaves
½   teaspoon sea salt
2   tablespoons lime juice

SALAD DRESSING
¼   cup fresh cilantro leaves
3   garlic cloves, crushed
⅓   cup lime juice, squeezed fresh
¾   cup olive oil
2   teaspoons honey
½   jalapeño, minced

FISH TACOS
3   pounds fresh halibut (1" thick)
3   tablespoons dry grill rub
Canola oil spray

5:30 TO 6:00 PM	GUESTS ARRIVE
	Read recipes and Team Plan.
6:00 TO 7:00 PM	**PREPARE APPETIZERS AND ENJOY WHILE YOU COOK**
6:00 TO 6:30	PICO DE GALLO • Prepare vegetables. • Mix and serve. TOMATILLO SALSA • Prepare vegetables. • Process. • Mix and serve.
6:30 TO 7:00	BAJA SALAD • Prepare salad dressing.
7:00 TO 7:30 PM	ENJOY SALAD
7:30 TO 8:00	FISH TACOS • Prepare fish. • Grill and serve.
8:00 TO 9:00 PM	ENJOY ENTRÉE
9:15 PM	ENJOY DESSERT

WORKSTATION:
Counter area
Grill

TOOLS:
Knife
Cutting Board
Fork or 2 spoons
Bowl
Juicer
2-quart saucepan
Wooden spoon
Measuring cups
Measuring spoons
Grill tongs

Kitchen towel
Cake server
Ice cream scoop

INGREDIENTS:
CITRUS GUACAMOLE
6   large, ripe avacados
3   tablespoons cilantro leaves
½   small red onion, chopped
3   cloves garlic, crushed
1   jalapeño, minced
½   orange
½   lime
1   teaspoon salt

MEXICAN RICE
2   tablespoons olive oil
½   yellow onion, chopped
3   cloves garlic, crushed
2   cups long grain rice
1   32-ounce. box organic chicken broth
2   teaspoons salt
1   12-ounce jar roasted red peppers, chopped
2   tablespoons parsley, chopped

TORTILLAS
16 Corn tortillas

5:30 TO 6:00 PM	GUESTS ARRIVE
	Read recipes and Team Plan.
6:00 TO 7:00 PM	PREPARE APPETIZERS AND ENJOY WHILE YOU COOK
6:00 TO 6:30	CITRUS GUACAMOLE • Prepare avocados. • Mix and serve.
6:30 TO 7:00	MEXICAN RICE • Sauté vegetables.
7:00 TO 7:30 PM	ENJOY SALAD
7:30 TO 8:00	MEXICAN RICE • Cook rice. FISH TACOS • Heat tortillas.
8:00 TO 9:00 PM	ENJOY ENTRÉE
9:00 TO 9:15	• Serve cake. (Team D to assist.)
9:15 PM	ENJOY DESSERT

A TASTE OF BAJA

WORKSTATION:
Oven
Counter area

TOOLS:
Microwave safe bowl
Mixer
Large mixer bowl
Measuring cups
Measuring spoons
Bowl
Sifter
Spatula
Springform pan
Collander
2-quart saucepan
Large spoon

INGREDIENTS:
CHOCOLATE CHIPOTLE BROWNIE CAKE
Butter and flour for cake pan
¾ cup butter
6 ounces semi-sweet chocolate, chips or pieces
4 ozs. unsweetened chocolate, chips or pieces
4 large eggs
¾ cup sugar
½ cup brown sugar
2 teaspoons vanilla extract
1½ teaspoons chipotle powder
¼ teaspoon cayenne pepper
1 teaspoon cinnamon
1 cup all-purpose flour
½ cup raisins, soaked overnight in beer, drained
½ cup hazelnuts, chopped and toasted
Powdered sugar for garnish
Vanilla ice cream, if desired
Espresso (optional)

BLACK BEANS WITH QUESO AÑEJO
2 15-ounce cans black beans
1 tablespoon olive oil
1 onion, finely chopped
4 garlic cloves, crushed
½ teaspoon ground cumin
1 14½-ounce can organic chicken broth
Salt and pepper to taste
½ cup queso añejo

5:30 TO 6:00 PM	GUESTS ARRIVE
	Read recipes and Team Plan.
6:00 TO 7:00 PM	**PREPARE APPETIZERS AND ENJOY WHILE YOU COOK**
6:00 TO 6:30	CHOCOLATE CHIPOTLE CAKE • Prepare cake pan and preheat oven. • Prepare cake batter.
6:30 TO 7:00	• Combine ingredients for cake.
7:00 TO 7:30 PM	**ENJOY SALAD**
7:30 TO 8:00	BLACK BEANS WITH QUESO AÑEJO • Drain black beans. • Cook beans. • Season beans and serve. CHOCOLATE CHIPOTLE BROWNIE CAKE • Bake cake.
8:00 TO 9:00 PM	**ENJOY ENTRÉE**
9:00 TO 9:15	• Serve cake. (Team C to assist.)
9:15 PM	**ENJOY DESSERT**

dinner
IN ATHENS

This menu transports you and your guests to the sun-kissed land of Greece for the evening. The warm Mediterranean climate produces the best olive and lemon trees, and this authentic menu capitalizes on them. ❧ Oregano, a mainstay of Greek cooking, gives a pungent aroma and flavor to the feta appetizer, the chicken souvlaki, grilled lamb chops, and the lemony roasted potatoes. Your guests will learn the magic of making tiropita cheese pastries by folding layers of buttered phyllo dough over a feta-ricotta filling. ❧ Lamb is the traditional meat served for special Greek celebrations. Here, it is treated to a flavorful spice rub before grilling. Chicken kabobs, or souvlaki, are marinated in lemon and yogurt for juicy tenderness and then grilled on skewers along with peppers and onions. ❧ Cool, creamy tzatziki, served with the homemade pita bread as an appetizer, also becomes an accompaniment to the souvlaki. ❧ For the finale, Glyka or "spoon sweets," combine the tang of Greek yogurt with the richness of dates and caramelized walnuts, drizzled with honey.

menu

APPETIZERS

Feta and Olives, Extra Virgin Olive Oil and Oregano

Homemade Pita Bread with Tzatziki

Grilled Asparagus

Tiropita

SALAD

Greek Salad

ENTRÉE

Chicken Souvlaki with Peppers and Onions, served with Tzatziki

Grilled Lamb Chops

Roasted Greek Potatoes with Oregano and Lemon

DESSERT

Glyka (Spoon Sweets) Greek Yogurt with Caramelized Walnuts, Dates and Honey

Baklava (optional)

MENU FOR EIGHT

Four Teams of Two
Team A
Team B
Team C
Team D
Total Preparation Time
Before Main Course
2 ½ Hours

Dinner in Athens
Cook the Part
May 25, 2010

Starters
Feta and Olives, Extra Virgin Olive Oil and Oregano
Grilled Asparagus
Homemade Pita Bread with Tzatziki
Tiropita

Salad
Greek Salad

Cook the Part
BARBARA

KARIN

feta and olives

Purchase high-quality olives, feta cheese and Greek olive oil at a European deli or gourmet market.

2 cups olives, any combination of the following:
Black and red kalamata olives
Green olives
Cretan olives
Black olives

1½ pounds feta cheese
Olive oil for drizzling
Fresh oregano, finely chopped
Crackers or sliced baguette

Host to prepare appetizers 1 hour ahead.

HOST **1.** *Prepare appetizer.*
Cube the feta, drizzle with olive oil and sprinkle with oregano.
Serve olives in decorative bowls.

Have some crackers or a sliced baguette available until the pita bread is ready.

SERVES 8

homemade pita bread

1⅛ cup very warm water
3 cups bread flour
1 teaspoon salt
1 tablespoon honey
2 teaspoons active dry yeast
2 tablespoons olive oil
Flour for rolling out dough
Olive oil for rubbing dough

Host to make pita dough early in the day.

HOST **1.** *Prepare dough.*
Put all ingredients into bread machine set on "dough setting." The dough will be ready in approximately 1 hour 40 minutes.

Remove dough from machine, rub with olive oil, place in a large resealable bag and refrigerate until 30 minutes before baking.

TEAM C **2.** *Bake pita bread.*
Heat oven to 450°.

Take the dough out of the refrigerator, divide it into 8 parts and roll each part into a ball. Let dough balls rest for 15 minutes.

Lightly flour a work surface. Flatten each ball into a circle, lightly sprinkling flour on the tops of the dough circles to allow for easy rolling. Roll each ball into a circle about 8" in diameter and ¼" thick.

Place 2 pita circles on a large baking sheet. Bake for 3½ minutes until they are puffy and only very lightly browned in spots. Repeat.

Cool on wire rack.

MAKES 8 PITA ROUNDS

tzatziki

1 ½ cucumbers
1 teaspoon sea salt
6 cloves garlic, crushed
4 tablespoons olive oil
2 cups plain Greek yogurt

The tzatziki will be served as an appetizer with the pita bread and will also be served later with the Chicken Souvlaki. After preparing the tzatziki, divide it into 2 small attractive serving bowls, cover and refrigerate until ready to serve.

TEAM B   **1.** *Prepare cucumbers for Tzatziki.*

Peel, seed and finely dice cucumbers.

Place cucumbers in a large strainer, toss with the salt and allow to drain for 15 minutes, squeezing them periodically with a spoon.

TEAM B   **2.** *Mix Tzatziki ingredients.*

Mix the drained cucumbers with the remaining ingredients and chill in 2 attractive serving bowls until ready to serve with appetizers and later with the chicken.

SERVES 8 – 12

grilled asparagus

1 pound pencil asparagus
Olive oil
½ teaspoon garlic salt
½ teaspoon kosher salt
½ lemon

TEAM D   **1.** *Prepare asparagus for grilling.*

Preheat grill.

Wash asparagus and trim off hard bottom ends (about 1").

Pat dry with paper towels.

Spray or brush asparagus with olive oil.

TEAM D   **2.** *Grill asparagus.*

Grill asparagus on a grill pan for 5 to 6 minutes or until tender and lightly browned.

Place asparagus in an attractive serving dish and sprinkle with garlic salt and kosher salt.

Squeeze juice of ½ lemon over grilled asparagus.

SERVES 8

tiropita

TIROPITA

1	1-pound box phyllo dough
½	pound butter

CHEESE FILLING

2	eggs
½	pound feta cheese
½	pound ricotta cheese
1	teaspoon dried dill
½	teaspoon salt
¼	teaspoon black pepper

TEAM A   **1.** *Prepare filling.*

Preheat oven to 350°.

Beat eggs and combine the cheese filling ingredients.

TEAM A   **2.** *Make Tiropita.*

& TEAM B   Melt butter in a small bowl in microwave on 50% power (about 90 seconds).

Remove 1 sheet of phyllo dough at a time, keeping the others covered with a damp cloth (otherwise they dry out and become brittle).

Brush the sheet with melted butter.

Fold it into thirds the long way by folding up the bottom third and folding down the top third.

Place a teaspoon of filling in the upper corner of the strip of dough.

Fold the top corner down over the filling. Continue folding triangles until the dough is used.

Bake triangles on a baking sheet for 11 to 12 minutes until golden brown.

MAKES APPROXIMATELY 40

Freeze any leftover triangles for later baking. Do not thaw before baking.

greek salad

GREEK SALAD

1	head romaine lettuce
1	head butter lettuce
1	cup red grape tomatoes
1	green pepper
½	cucumber
1	cup pitted kalamata olives

GREEK SALAD DRESSING

1	lemon
½	cup olive oil
1	teaspoon Worchestershire sauce
½	cup feta cheese, cut into small cubes
1	teaspoon finely chopped fresh oregano

Freshly ground pepper

Salt to taste

TEAM A   **1.** *Prepare vegetables for salad.*

Wash lettuces, spin dry and tear into large pieces.

Wash tomatoes and drain.

Core green pepper and chop into ½" pieces.

Peel and thinly slice cucumber.

Place all ingredients serving bowl.

TEAM D   **2.** *Prepare salad dressing.*

Squeeze juice from lemon into jar. Add remaining ingredients and shake to combine.

TEAM A   **3.** *Toss salad and serve.*

SERVES 8

chicken souvlaki

5   skinless, boneless chicken
     breasts

2   green peppers

2   red onions

MARINADE

1   lemon

1½ cups nonfat plain yogurt

3   garlic cloves, crushed

1   tablespoon fresh oregano,
     chopped

1   teaspoon salt

Freshly ground pepper

Olive oil for brushing vegetables

TEAM B   **1.** *Cut up chicken and vegetables.*

Cut chicken into 1½" cubes.

Cut green peppers into 2" pieces.

Cut red onions into quarters and then divide each quarter in half.

TEAM C   **2.** *Prepare marinade for chicken.*

Squeeze lemon into large glass bowl. Add remaining ingredients and stir.

TEAM C   **3.** *Marinate chicken.*

Mix the chicken with the marinade, cover with plastic wrap and chill until 15 minutes before grilling.

TEAM C   **4.** *Prepare skewers.* *

Put chicken on skewers, leaving a small amount of space between pieces. Skewer peppers and onions, each on its own skewer, with some space between the pieces. Brush the vegetables with olive oil. Place skewers on large baking sheets to take to grill.

TEAM D   **5.** *Grill chicken and vegetables.*

Heat grill to medium. Grill the vegetable skewers until the vegetables are tender and a little browned. Remove from skewers to a large serving bowl and keep warm in a warming drawer or pre-warmed oven.

Grill chicken skewers on medium until the chicken is done, about 10 minutes total, turning periodically. Remove from skewers and add to the serving bowl with vegetables.

Serve with tzatziki.

SERVES 8

*You can use grill racks instead of the skewers. Using grill racks will result in more even grilling.

grilled lamb chops

RUB

1	tablespoon kosher salt
1	tablespoon ground black pepper
1	tablespoon dried oregano
2	teaspoons garlic powder
2	teaspoons onion powder
1	teaspoon smoked paprika
½	teaspoon celery seeds
16	lamb rib chops (2 racks of lamb)

Lemon wedges

TEAM D   **1. *Mix rub.***

Combine all spices in a small bowl.

TEAM A   **2. *Prepare chops and chill.***

Cut each rack of lamb into 8 pieces.

Dip each of the chops into the rub mixture, coating evenly on each side. Shake or brush off excess rub. Place chops in 9" x 13" inch glass pan and chill until ready to grill.

TEAM D   **3. *Grill chops.***

Heat grill to medium high. Grill chops for approximately 4 to 6 minutes per side for medium.

Serve with lemon wedges.

SERVES 8

roasted greek potatoes with oregano and lemon

5	pounds russet potatoes
1	lemon
½	cup olive oil
2	tablespoons fresh oregano, finely chopped
4	cloves garlic, crushed
2	teaspoons kosher salt

HOST   **1. *Prep potatoes.***

Peel potatoes, wash, cut into long wedges (4 to 6 depending on size of potato) and cover with cold water.

TEAM C   **2. *Dry, season and roast potatoes.***

Preheat oven to 425°.

Dry potatoes using paper towels.

Squeeze lemon juice into small bowl.

Add olive oil, oregano and garlic. Stir to combine.

Spread potatoes out in a single layer in a large metal roasting pan. Pour olive oil mixture over potatoes and toss. Sprinkle potatoes with kosher salt. Roast until browned and tender, 50 to 60 minutes, turning every 15 minutes to make sure they don't stick to the pan. Keep warm until ready to serve.

SERVES 8 - 12

glyka (spoon sweets)

GREEK YOGURT WITH CARAMELIZED WALNUTS, DATES AND HONEY

1	tablespoon butter
1 ½	cups walnut halves
1	tablespoon honey for caramelizing walnuts
1 ½	cups pitted dates
2 ⅔	cups plain Greek yogurt
½	cup honey*

*Best with a high quality honey from a Greek grocery.

HOST **1. Caramelize walnuts.**

Melt butter in a skillet and add walnuts. Saute until walnuts begin to brown. Add honey and mix into walnuts until they caramelize.

TEAM B **2. Slice dates.**

TEAM A **3. Prepare yogurt for serving.**

Place ⅓ cup yogurt on each of eight plates.

Divide the dates and walnuts over the yogurt.

Drizzle with honey and serve.

SERVES 8

baklava (optional)

Host to prepare this optional dessert up to 2 weeks ahead.

SYRUP

2	cups sugar
1	cup honey
2	cups water
Zest of 1 lemon	
2	cinnamon sticks

FILLING

4	cups nuts (walnuts or pecans)
1	cup sugar
3	teaspoons cinnamon
1 ½	teaspoons nutmeg
2	1-pound boxes phyllo dough
1	pound butter, melted

Baklava cutting diagram

HOST **1. Prepare syrup.**

Combine all syrup ingredients in saucepan and boil for 30 minutes.

2. Prepare filling.

Place all filling ingredients in bowl of food processor and process until mixture is well blended and nuts are finely chopped.

3. Assemble baklava.

Remove 1 sheet of phyllo dough at a time, keeping the others covered with a damp cloth (otherwise they dry out and become brittle).

Brush butter onto a large round pizza pan with a 1" rim. Place a sheet of phyllo dough into the bottom of the pan. Cover entire pan with dough. Brush the dough with melted butter. Repeat 8 times, brushing each layer with butter.

Sprinkle ½ cup of nut filling evenly over dough, then add 3 layers of dough, brushing butter between each layer. Repeat 8 to 10 times until the pan is full and the nut mixture and dough are used up.

Cut off overhanging dough and finish off by creating a rim around the edge, folding inward and tucking in the dough to create an edge.

Cut the baklava as shown in the diagram, creating diamonds.

4. Bake the baklava.

Bake at 300° for 1½ hours, covering with foil after the first hour.

Remove from oven and cool.

5. Finish.

Pour hot syrup over the cold baklava.

Cut the baklava all the way through to separate diamonds. Place each diamond into paper petit four cups for serving.

master PLAN

host preparation

Follow *Host Prep Guidelines* on page 17.

For this menu, follow the **HOST** instructions for the following recipes:
Up to 2 weeks ahead . . . *Baklava* (optional dessert)
Early in the day . . . . *Pita Bread* (prepare dough)
Early in the day . . . . *Glyka* (caramelize walnuts)
2 hours ahead . . . . *Roasted Greek Potatoes* (prep potatoes)
1 hour ahead . . . . *Feta and Olives*

5:30 TO 6:00 PM	GUESTS ARRIVE — HOST PROVIDES GUEST ORIENTATION — PAGE 17

	TEAM A	TEAM B	TEAM C	TEAM D
6:00 TO 7:30 PM	**PREPARE APPETIZERS AND ENJOY WHILE YOU COOK**			
6:00 TO 7:00	• Prepare tiropita filling. • Make half of the tiropita. (Team B will make half of the tiropita.)	• Prepare cucumbers for tzatziki. • Mix tzatziki ingredients. • Make half of the tiropita. (Team A has made filling and has tools.)	• Bake pita bread. • Dry, season and roast potatoes.	• Prepare and grill asparagus. • Mix rub for chops. (Give rub to Team A.)
7:00 TO 7:30	• Prepare chops and chill. (Get rub from Team D.) • Prepare vegetables for salad. (Get dressing from Team D.) • Toss salad and serve.	• Cut up chicken and vegetables. (Give to Team C to marinate.)	• Prepare marinade for chicken. • Marinate chicken. • Prepare skewers.	• Prepare salad dressing. (Give dressing to Team A.)
7:30 TO 8:00 PM	**ENJOY SALAD**			
8:00 TO 8:30		• Slice dates. (Give to Team A.)		• Grill chops, chicken and vegetables.
8:30 TO 9:30 PM	**ENJOY ENTRÉE**			
9:30 TO 9:45	• Prepare yogurt for serving. (Get sliced dates from Team B.)	• Prepare coffee and serve.		
9:45 PM	**ENJOY DESSERT**			

WORKSTATION:
Oven
Counter area

TOOLS:
Medium bowl (filling)
Measuring spoons
Measuring cups
Fork
Mixing spoon
Small bowl (butter)
Damp cloth
Pastry brush
Spatula
Baking sheet

Large knife
Cutting board
9" x 13" glass pan
Salad spinner
Paring knife
Vegetable peeler
Drizzle spoon

INGREDIENTS:
TIROPITA
1   1-pound box phyllo dough
½   pound butter

CHEESE FILLING
2   eggs
½   pound feta cheese
½   pound ricotta cheese
1   teaspoon dried dill
½   teaspoon salt
¼   teaspoon black pepper

GRILLED LAMB CHOPS
16 lamb rib chops (2 racks of lamb)

GREEK SALAD
1   head Romaine lettuce
1   head butter lettuce

1   cup red grape tomatoes
1   green pepper
½   cucumber
1   cup pitted kalamata olives

GLYKA (SPOON SWEETS)
2⅔ cups plain Greek yogurt
1½ cups caramelized walnut halves
½   cup honey

5:30 TO 6:00 PM	GUESTS ARRIVE
	Read recipes and Team Plan.
6:00 TO 7:30 PM	PREPARE APPETIZERS AND ENJOY WHILE YOU COOK
6:00 TO 7:00	TIROPITA • Prepare tiropita. • Make half of the tiropita. (Team B will make half of the tiropita.)
7:00 TO 7:30	GRILLED LAMB CHOPS • Prepare chops and chill. (Get rub from Team D.) GREEK SALAD • Prepare vegetables for salad. (Get dressing from Team D.) • Toss salad and serve.
7:30 TO 8:00 PM	ENJOY SALAD
8:30 TO 9:30 PM	ENJOY ENTRÉE
9:30 TO 9:45	GLYKA (SPOON SWEETS) • Prepare yogurt for serving. (Get sliced dates from Team B.)
9:45 PM	ENJOY DESSERT

WORKSTATION:
Counter area
Oven

TOOLS:
Vegetable peeler
Strainer
Measuring spoons
Measuring cups
Mixing spoon
Mixing bowl
Poultry knife
Paring knife
Cutting board

INGREDIENTS:
TZATZIKI
1½ cucumbers
1 teaspoon sea salt
6 cloves garlic, crushed
4 tablespoons olive oil
2 cups plain Greek yogurt

CHICKEN SOUVLAKI
5 skinless, boneless chicken breasts
2 green peppers
2 red onions

GLYKA (SPOON SWEETS)
1½ cups pitted dates

5:30 TO 6:00 PM	GUESTS ARRIVE
	Read recipes and Team Plan.
6:00 TO 7:30 PM	PREPARE APPETIZERS AND ENJOY WHILE YOU COOK
6:00 TO 7:00	TZATZIKI • Prepare cucumbers for tzatziki. • Mix tzatziki ingredients. TIROPITA • Make half of the tiropita. (Team A has made the filling and has tools.)
7:00 TO 7:30	CHICKEN SOUVLAKI • Cut up chicken and vegetables. (Give to Team C to marinate.)
7:30 TO 8:00 PM	ENJOY SALAD
8:00 TO 8:30	GLYKA (SPOON SWEETS) • Slice dates. (Give to Team A.)
8:30 TO 9:30 PM	ENJOY ENTRÉE
9:30 TO 9:45	Prepare coffee and serve.
9:45 PM	ENJOY DESSERT

TEAM C

WORKSTATION:
Oven
Counter area

TOOLS:
Rolling pin
Baking sheets
Cooling wire rack
Paper towels
Small bowl
Measuring cups
Measuring spoons
Knife
Juicer

Large metal roasting pan
Large glass bowl
Plastic wrap
Skewers or grill racks
Pastry brush

INGREDIENTS:
HOMEMADE PITA BREAD
Dough
Flour for rolling out dough

ROASTED GREEK
POTATOES WITH
OREGANO AND LEMON
Prepped potatoes
1   lemon
½   cup olive oil
2   tablespoons fresh
     oregano, finely chopped
4   cloves garlic, crushed
2   teaspoons kosher salt

CHICKEN SOUVLAKI
MARINADE
1   lemon
1 ½ cups nonfat plain
     yogurt
3   garlic cloves, crushed
1   tablespoon fresh
     oregano, chopped
1   teaspoon salt
Freshly ground pepper
Olive oil for brushing
vegetables

5:30 TO 6:00 PM	GUESTS ARRIVE
	Read recipes and Team Plan.
6:00 TO 7:30 PM	**PREPARE APPETIZERS AND ENJOY WHILE YOU COOK**
6:00 TO 7:00	HOMEMADE PITA BREAD • Bake pita bread. ROASTED GREEK POTATOES WITH OREGANO AND LEMON • Dry, season and roast potatoes.
7:00 TO 7:30	CHICKEN SOUVLAKI • Prepare marinade for chicken. (Get cut up chicken and vegetables from Team B.) • Marinate chicken. • Prepare skewers.
7:30 TO 8:00 PM	ENJOY SALAD
8:30 TO 9:30 PM	ENJOY ENTRÉE
9:45 PM	ENJOY DESSERT

WORKSTATION:
Grill
Counter area

TOOLS:
Knife
Cutting board
Paper towels
Pastry brush
Grill pan
Grill tongs
Small bowl (rub)
Measuring spoons
Jar (dressing)
Measuring cups

Juicer
Spoon
Large fork
Grill racks
Spatula
Grill tongs

INGREDIENTS:
GRILLED ASPARAGUS
1   pound pencil asparagus
Olive oil
½ teaspoon garlic salt
½ teaspoon kosher salt
½ lemon

RUB FOR LAMB CHOPS
1   tablespoon kosher salt
1   tablespoon ground black pepper
1   tablespoon dried oregano
2   teaspoons garlic powder
2   teaspoons onion powder
1   teaspoon smoked paprika
½ teaspoon celery seeds
Lemon wedges

GREEK SALAD DRESSING
1   lemon
½ cup olive oil
1   teaspoon Worchestershire sauce
½ cup feta cheese, cut into small cubes
1   teaspoon finely chopped fresh oregano
Freshly ground pepper
Salt to taste

5:30 TO 6:00 PM	GUESTS ARRIVE
	Read recipes and Team Plan.
6:00 TO 7:30 PM	PREPARE APPETIZERS AND ENJOY WHILE YOU COOK
6:00 TO 7:00	GRILLED ASPARAGUS • Prepare and grill asparagus. GRILLED LAMB CHOPS Mix rub for chops. (Give rub to Team A.)
7:00 TO 7:30	GREEK SALAD • Prepare salad dressing. (Give dressing to Team A.)
7:30 TO 8:00 PM	ENJOY SALAD
8:00 TO 8:30	GRILLED LAMB CHOPS • Grill chops. CHICKEN SOUVLAKI • Grill chicken and vegetables.
8:30 TO 9:30 PM	ENJOY ENTRÉE
9:45 PM	ENJOY DESSERT

spanish WINE DINNER

This menu captures the Spaniards' love of food and the diversity of their ingredients, such as olives, figs, Manchego cheese, fresh vegetables and seafood. The meal begins with tapas of piquant Spanish olives, crostini topped with sweet fig jam and shaved Manchego cheese, potato omelet, and crispy deep-fried calamari. Traditionally, these "small plates" help carry over the Spanish until their typical dinner hour at 10 or 11 in the evening. In this menu, the small plates play the role of appetizers to stimulate the palette before the meal. ❧ Vodka-laced gazpacho is followed by the Spanish signature dish—Paella a la Valenciana. The huge pan of rice, brimming with shellfish, sausage, chicken and colorful peppers, steals the show. ❧ It is difficult to finish off this meal with only one dessert. The velvety flan is prepared ahead of time by the host. The rich hazelnut torta, prepared by the guests, is served with whipped cream and a tart raspberry coulis. ❧ You can use the suggested wines, or seek out alternatives at your favorite wine store. Use bold, red napkins to capture the essence of the Spanish table!

menu

APPETIZERS (TAPAS)

Mixed Marinated Spanish Olives

Crostini with Fig Jam and Shaved Manchego Cheese

Tortilla Española

Calamari Fritti with Spanish Tomato Sauce

SOUP

Vodka-Laced Gazpacho

ENTRÉE

Paella a la Valenciana with Crusty Bread

DESSERT

Mini Flan

Hazelnut Chocolate Torta with Whipped Cream

MENU FOR EIGHT

Four Teams of Two
Team A
Team B
Team C
Team D
Total Preparation Time
Before Main Course
2 ½ Hours

The Host will take primary responsibility for the Tapas. Two tasks will be assigned to teams: the final step for the Tortilla Española and the final step of the Calamari Fritti. The recipes are marked accordingly.

mixed marinated spanish olives

2 cups Mixed Spanish Olives

Olives can be purchased at your local gourmet market.

Host to prepare 1 hour before guests arrive.

HOST **1.** *Prepare appetizer.*
Place olives in a serving bowl to serve with other tapas.

crostini with fig jam and shaved manchego cheese

1 baguette, sliced ¼" thick
Olive oil to brush bread slices
Fig jam, purchased (can be found at a gourmet market)
½ pound Manchego cheese, sliced thin

Host to prepare up to 3 hours before guests arrive.

HOST **1.** *Prep crostini.*
Preheat oven to 400°.
Place bread slices on baking sheet and brush with olive oil.
Bake for approximately 6 minutes.
Turn and bake an additional 5 to 6 minutes. Set aside to cool.

HOST **2.** *Finish preparing crostini 1 hour before guests arrive.*
Spread crostini with fig jam and top with a slice of Manchego cheese.
Place on a platter to serve with other tapas.

wines

· · · · · · ·

APPETIZERS (TAPAS)
🍇 *Gran Reserva Brut Cava or Amontillado Sherry* 🍇

SOUP
🍇 *Tempranillo or White Rioja* 🍇

ENTRÉE (PAELLA)
🍇 *Rioja Alavesa Gran Reserva or Rioja Alta Gran Reserva* 🍇

DESSERT
🍇 *Pedro Ximenez Sherry* 🍇

· · · · · · ·

tortilla española

4 tablespoons Spanish olive oil, divided

4 Yukon Gold potatoes, sliced very thin (use a mandolin, if available, set at 1/8")

2 teaspoons kosher salt

1 onion, cut in half and sliced very thin

2 garlic cloves, crushed

6 large eggs

1 teaspoon kosher salt

2 teaspoons dry grill rub or Gary's Rub*

Freshly ground pepper to taste

Roasted red pepper strips, purchased or homemade

*Recipe on page 26.

Host to prepare potatoes 1 hour before guests arrive. Team C to finish.

HOST
1. *Prepare potatoes for Tortilla Española.*

Heat 2 tablespoons oil in large nonstick skillet on medium-high heat.

Add potato slices and sauté for 12 minutes, turning to ensure even cooking.

Add another tablespoon oil and 1 teaspoon salt. Reduce flame to medium.

Add onions and continue cooking until onions are soft and potatoes are tender, about 5 minutes.

Add crushed garlic and sauté for 2 minutes. Turn off heat and set aside.

TEAM C
2. *Prepare eggs and finish Tortilla Española. Serve.*

Beat eggs with 1 teaspoon salt, Gary's Rub and pepper in a large bowl.

Remove potatoes from skillet, add to egg mixture and let stand for 10 minutes.

Add 1 tablespoon oil to skillet. Pour egg and potato mixture into heated skillet.

Allow eggs to set, lifting the sides of the omelet to let more egg mixture run underneath to cook.

When the omelet can be lifted from the side of the pan, invert it onto a plate and slide back into the pan to cook the other side. Add ground pepper to taste.

Slide the cooked omelet onto a cutting board or serving plate and cut into cubes or wedges. This can be served at room temperature. Serve with roasted red peppers strips.

SERVES 8

calamari fritti with spanish tomato sauce

2 pounds squid tubes

2 cups buttermilk

Canola oil for deep frying

3 cups all-purpose flour

2 tablespoons Gary's Rub*

2 teaspoons kosher salt

1 teaspoon garlic salt

1 teaspoon freshly ground black pepper

2 lemons, cut into quarters

*Recipe on page 26.

SPANISH TOMATO SAUCE

1 pound fresh tomatoes or a 28-ounce can plum tomatoes with juice*

6 garlic cloves

1 cup onion, chopped

½ teaspoon red pepper flakes

¼ cup Spanish olive oil

Salt and pepper to taste

*If you use canned tomatoes, add 1 teaspoon sugar

Host to prep calamari 3 hours before guests arrive and to prepare tomato sauce up to 1 day in advance. Simply reheat before serving.

HOST   **1.** *Prep the calamari.*

Rinse squid and pat dry. Cut into ½" rings.

Cover with buttermilk and refrigerate 1 to 2 hours.

Mix flour, Gary's Rub, salts and pepper in a bowl. Set aside to use later to coat the calamari.

HOST   **2.** *Prepare Spanish Tomato Sauce.*

Process tomatoes in a food processor. Add garlic and chopped onion. Blend. Add red pepper flakes.

While the processor is running, add the Spanish olive oil. Season with salt and freshly ground pepper to taste.

Pour the mixture into a saucepan over medium heat and simmer for 15 minutes. Pour into a bowl to serve with the calamari.

TEAM D   **2.** *Fry calamari. Serve.*

Heat oil to 375° in deep fryer or large pot.

Toss the calamari in the flour mixture to coat.

Drop calamari into heated oil and allow to cook until golden brown (6 to 8 minutes).

Remove with a slotted spoon to a platter lined with paper towels.

Allow to drain and then transfer to a serving platter with the tomato sauce and lemon wedges.

SERVES 8 - 10

vodka-laced gazpacho

2	large red tomatoes, quartered
1	large cucumber, peeled and halved
1	onion, halved
1	green pepper, halved
1	pimiento, drained
24	ounces organic tomato juice
⅓	cup Spanish olive oil
½	cup red wine vinegar
1 ½	teaspoons salt
½	teaspoon Tabasco sauce
1	garlic clove, crushed
½	cup vodka
6	tablespoons olive oil
1	garlic clove
1	loaf Italian or Vienna bread (preferably one day old), cut into ½" cubes
¼	cup chives, chopped

Host to prepare 1 day ahead.

HOST **1. *Prepare soup for chilling.***

Combine tomatoes, ½ cucumber, ½ onion, ½ green pepper, pimiento and ½ cup tomato juice in food processor. Blend until vegetables are pureed.

Pour the pureed mixture into a large glass bowl or pitcher and add the remaining tomato juice, olive oil, red wine vinegar, salt, Tabasco sauce and crushed garlic clove.

Add the vodka and chill.

HOST **2. *Chill 8 bowls for serving the soup.***

HOST **3. *Prepare croutons.***

Heat 3 tablespoons olive oil in a large skillet.

Add garlic clove and cook for 1 minute. Discard garlic clove.

Add bread cubes to skillet and brown, adding more oil as required.

Remove browned croutons and add remaining cubes until all croutons are nicely browned. Place in a small bowl to serve.

TEAM A **4. *Finish and serve Gazpacho.***

Chop the ½ cucumber, ½ onion, and ½ green pepper. Place in small bowls for guests to add to the chilled soup along with the chives and croutons.

SERVES 8

paella a la valenciana

6	slices thick bacon	
8	tablespoons Spanish olive oil, divided	
2	large onions, chopped	
1	Anaheim chili pepper, seeded and chopped	
1	jalapeño, seeded and minced	
1	red bell pepper, seeded and chopped	
1	yellow bell pepper, seeded and chopped	
1	green bell pepper, seeded and chopped	
8	garlic cloves, crushed	
4	cups medium grain rice	
2	teaspoons kosher salt	

2	32-ounce boxes organic chicken broth
1	teaspoon saffron threads
1	12-ounce bottle clam juice
1	tablespoon coarsely ground black pepper
3	ripe tomatoes, finely chopped
¼	cup fresh thyme, chopped
½	cup red wine
16	clams, scrubbed
16	mussels, scrubbed and debearded
24	large shrimp (16 to 20 count per pound), peeled and deveined, tails on

1	10-ounce package frozen peas
2	tablespoons Gary's Rub*
2	pounds boneless skinless chicken breasts, rinsed and dried
1	pound smoked sausage
2	large lobsters, cooked, cleaned and rinsed
½	cup Italian parsley, chopped
1	4-ounce jar pimientos, drained
2	lemons, quartered

*Recipe on page 26.

TEAM A   **1.** *Prepare paella on the stovetop.*

In large paella pan, sauté the bacon until brown.

Remove from pan, drain, crumble and reserve. Add a few tablespoons of olive oil to the bacon grease.

Add onions and sauté until sweated.

Add all the chopped peppers and garlic. Sauté a few minutes more until soft.

Add a bit more olive oil and then add the rice and salt. Stir until rice is nicely coated with the oil.

Heat the broth in a saucepan.

In a small cup, moisten the saffron threads in some of the broth. Slowly add remaining broth and saffon to the paella pan.

Add the clam juice. Cover and cook rice for 10 minutes.

Add the ground pepper, chopped tomatoes, thyme, and wine. Allow to cook until the rice is *al dente*, about 25 minutes, simmering on low heat. Avoid over-browning the rice on the bottom of the pan. (You may have to loosen it once or twice during cooking. "Soccarat," a crust, will form on the pan bottom. This is a natural part of your paella).

Add the clams, mussels, shrimp, peas and crumbled bacon. Cover completely with aluminum foil. Continue cooking until shrimp are completely cooked and mussels and clams are open (approximately 15 minutes).

TEAM B   **2.** *Grill chicken, sausage and lobster for paella.*

Heat grill to medium. Sprinkle the chicken with Gary's Rub. Grill chicken and smoked sausage until done and nicely browned. Cut sausage and chicken into bite-sized pieces. Remove meat to a platter, tent with foil and put into a warming drawer or oven until ready to add to the paella.

Brush cleaned lobsters with olive oil and grill until warm and lightly browned. Remove from shells, cut into serving-size pieces and reserve. Keep warm.

TEAM C   **3.** *Finish paella.*

Add chicken and sausage to paella pan. Cover and let stand 15 to 20 minutes. Add grilled lobster before serving.

Top with the parsley and pimientos and garnish with the lemon wedges.

Serve with crusty bread.

SERVES 8 - 10

mini flan

1 ½ cups sugar
½ cup water
1 ¾ cups whipping cream
1 cup whole milk
½ vanilla bean
5 eggs
5 tablespoons sugar

Host to prepare up to 2 days ahead.

HOST **1.** *Prepare the caramel.*

Preheat oven to 350°.

Put the water in a 1½ quart saucepan. Bring water to boil over medium heat and add sugar. Stir to dissolve sugar. When the sugar is dissolved, turn heat to high and cover the pot, stirring at 2 minute intervals. Swirl the pan occasionally. Continue this process until the sugar has become a smooth dark caramel, about 10 minutes.

Pour a tablespoon of caramel into each of 12 mini ramekins. Rotate the ramekins so that the caramel covers the bottom and partially up the sides.

HOST **2.** *Prepare custard.*

Combine cream and whole milk in a saucepan. Cover vanilla bean with hot water for a few minutes to plump. Cut bean in half lengthwise and scrape the inside, adding the scrapings and bean to the milk mixture. Bring to simmer.

Turn off heat and allow to cool. Discard scraped vanilla bean.

Blend eggs with sugar in a medium bowl using a whisk. Gradually add the cooled milk mixture to the eggs.

Fill the mini ramekins with the custard mixture and set into a large metal baking pan.

Fill the pan with boiling water about half way up the sides of the ramekins.

Bake until set—about 30 to 35 minutes. Remove ramekins from the pan and allow to cool.

Refrigerate for at least 2 hours.

TEAM C **3.** *Invert and serve.*

Run a sharp small knife around the flan to loosen the sides when ready to serve. Invert each ramekin onto a plate. Shake to release flan. Caramel will run over the flan. Serve with Hazelnut Chocolate Torta.

SERVES 12

hazelnut chocolate torta with whipped cream

Butter and flour to coat springform pan

9	ounces bittersweet chocolate
2	cups hazelnuts, chopped
18	tablespoons butter (2 sticks plus 2 tablespoons)
1 ⅓	cups sugar
6	eggs

Whipped cream

FRUIT COULIS (OPTIONAL)

12	ounces fresh raspberries
¼	cup sugar

HOST

1. *Prepare fruit coulis (if desired). Host to prepare up to 2 days ahead.*

Bring raspberries and sugar to boil in a small saucepan. Simmer for 15 minutes.

Pass raspberries through a strainer and pour coulis into a squeeze bottle. Discard strained seeds.

TEAM D

2. *Prepare batter.*

Preheat oven to 350°.

Butter and flour a 10" springform pan. Place a large piece of parchment paper across the bottom of the pan before clasping on the ring of the pan. The paper should extend outside of the ring. This will help when removing the cake after chilling.

Melt chocolate in microwave on medium power in a glass mixing bowl, starting with 1 minute and adding 30 second intervals until melted (about 2 minutes, 30 seconds total).

Mix hazelnuts into chocolate and cool mixture.

Cream butter in large bowl of electric mixer. Add sugar and mix until light and fluffy. Add the eggs, one at a time, until creamy.

Fold the cooled chocolate mixture into the creamed butter mixture until blended. Pour into the springform pan.

TEAM D

3. *Bake and chill.*

Bake the torta 35 to 45 minutes until the center is set but not dry.

Cool. Loosen pan by running a knife around the edge and remove ring. Finish cooling and then refrigerate until set.

TEAM D

4. *Serve.*

Cut into very thin slices and serve with whipped cream. Decorate with a fruit coulis, if desired. Serve with mini flan.

SERVES 12

master
PLAN

host preparation

Follow *Host Prep Guidelines* on page 17.

- Prepare Gary's Rub well in advance or purchase a dry grill rub to substitute.
- This menu has an extensive shopping list for ingredients and wine, so start planning and shopping early.
- Serve host-prepared appetizers as you review the plans. Each team can then take turns finishing and serving Tapas and Gazpacho. The following order is recommended: Tortilla Española, Calamari Fritti, Gazpacho.
- Add crusty bread to your shopping list.

For this menu, follow the **HOST** instructions for the following recipes:

Up to 2 days ahead . . .	*Hazelnut Chocolate Torta* (optional: prepare fruit coulis)
Up to 2 days ahead . . .	*Mini Flan*
1 day ahead	*Calamari Fritti* (Spanish Tomato Sauce)
1 day ahead	*Vodka-Laced Gazpacho*
3 hours ahead.	*Calamari Fritti* (prep calamari)
Up to 3 hours ahead . . .	*Crostini* (prep crostini)
1 hour ahead.	*Crostini* (finish crostini)
1 hour ahead.	*Tortilla Española* (prepare potatoes)
1 hour ahead.	*Mixed Marinated Spanish Olives*

5:30 TO 6:00 PM	GUESTS ARRIVE – HOST PROVIDES GUEST ORIENTATION – PAGE 17

	TEAM A	TEAM B	TEAM C	TEAM D
6:00 TO 7:30 PM	**FINISH PREPARING APPETIZERS AND ENJOY WHILE YOU COOK**			
6:00 TO 6:30		• Prepare wines and match to proper course throughout the evening.		• Fry Calamari. Serve.
6:15 TO 6:30			• Prepare eggs and finish Tortilla Española. Serve.	
6:30 TO 6:45	• Finish and serve Gazpacho.			
7:00 TO 7:30 PM	**ENJOY SOUP**			
7:30 TO 8:30	• Prepare Paella on the stovetop. (Team B will do grilling for Paella.)	• Grill chicken, sausage and lobster for Paella. (Give to Team C.)	• Finish Paella.	• Prepare batter for Hazelnut Choclate Torta. • Bake and chill.
8:30 TO 9:30 PM	**ENJOY ENTRÉE**			
9:30 TO 9:45			• Invert and serve Mini Flans. (Work with Team D to serve desserts.)	• Serve Hazelnut Chocolate Torta. (Team D will assist with serving dessert.)
9:45 PM	**ENJOY DESSERT**			

WORKSTATION:
Counter area
Stovetop

TOOLS:
Knife
Cutting board
Paella pan
Measuring spoons
Saucepan
Cup
Spoon
Spatula
Foil

INGREDIENTS:
FOR FINAL STEP AND
SERVING OF GAZPACHO
½ cucumber, peeled
½ onion
½ green pepper
¼ cup chives, chopped
Croutons

PAELLA
A LA VALENCIANA
6 slices thick bacon
8 tablespoons Spanish
 olive oil, divided
2 large onions, chopped
1 Anaheim chili pepper,
 seeded and chopped
1 jalapeño, seeded and
 minced

1 red bell pepper, seeded
 and chopped
1 yellow bell pepper,
 seeded and chopped
1 green bell pepper,
 seeded and chopped
8 garlic cloves, crushed
4 cups medium grain rice
2 teaspoons kosher salt
2 32-ounce boxes organic
 chicken broth
1 teaspoon saffron
 threads
1 12-ounce bottle clam
 juice
1 tablespoon coarsely
 ground black pepper
3 ripe tomatoes, finely
 chopped
¼ cup fresh thyme,
 chopped

½ cup red wine
16 clams, scrubbed
16 mussels, scrubbed and
 debearded
24 large shrimp (16 to 20
 count per pound),
 peeled and deveined,
 tails on
1 10-ounce package
 frozen peas

5:30 TO 6:00 PM	GUESTS ARRIVE
	Read recipes and Team Plan.
6:00 TO 7:00 PM	FINISH PREPARING APPETIZERS AND ENJOY WHILE YOU COOK
6:30 TO 6:45	VODKA-LACED GAZPACHO • Finish and serve Gazpacho.
7:00 TO 7:30 PM	ENJOY SOUP
7:30 TO 8:30	PAELLA A LA VALENCIANA • Prepare Paella on the stovetop. (Team B will do grilling for Paella.)
8:30 TO 9:30 PM	ENJOY ENTRÉE
9:45 PM	ENJOY DESSERT

SPANISH WINE DINNER

WORKSTATION:
Bar area
Grill

TOOLS:
Cork screw
Grill tools
Knife
Cutting board
Large platter
Foil
Pastry brush

INGREDIENTS:

PAELLA A LA VALENCIANA

2 tablespoons Gary's Rub

2 pounds boneless skinless chicken breasts, rinsed and dried

1 pound smoked sausage

2 large lobsters, cooked, cleaned and rinsed

Spanish olive oil

5:30 TO 6:00 PM	**GUESTS ARRIVE**
	Read recipes and Team Plan.
6:00 TO 7:00 PM	**FINISH PREPARING APPETIZERS AND ENJOY WHILE YOU COOK**
6:00 TO 6:30	• Prepare wines and match to proper course throughout the evening.
7:00 TO 7:30 PM	**ENJOY SOUP**
7:30 TO 8:30	PAELLA A LA VALENCIANA • Grill chicken, sausage and lobster for Paella. (Give to Team C.)
8:30 TO 9:30 PM	**ENJOY ENTRÉE**
9:45 PM	**ENJOY DESSERT**

WORKSTATION:
Counter area
Stovetop

TOOLS:
Bowl
Whisk
Measuring spoons
Spatula
Knife
Sharp small knife

INGREDIENTS:
TORTILLA ESPAÑOLA

6	large eggs
2	teaspoons Gary's Rub
1	teaspoon kosher salt
1	tablespoon Spanish olive oil

Freshly ground pepper to taste

Roasted red pepper strips, purchased or homemade

PAELLA A LA VALENCIANA

½	cup Italian parsley, chopped
1	4-ounce jar pimientos, drained
2	lemons, quartered

5:30 TO 6:00 PM	GUESTS ARRIVE
	Read recipes and Team Plan.
6:00 TO 7:00 PM	FINISH PREPARING APPETIZERS AND ENJOY WHILE YOU COOK
6:15 TO 6:30	TORTILLA ESPAÑOLA • Prepare eggs and finish Tortilla Española. Serve.
7:00 TO 7:30 PM	ENJOY SOUP
7:30 TO 8:30	PAELLA A LA VALENCIANA • Finish Paella.
8:30 TO 9:30 PM	ENJOY ENTRÉE
9:30 TO 9:45	MINI FLAN • Invert and serve. (Work with Team D to serve desserts.)
9:45 PM	ENJOY DESSERT

SPANISH WINE DINNER

WORKSTATION:
Counter area
Deep fry area
Oven

TOOLS:
Large rimmed pan
Deep fryer or large pot
Slotted spoon
Paper towels
Springform pan
Parchment paper
Glass mixing bowl
Measuring cups
Electric mixer
Spatula
Knife
Spoon

INGREDIENTS:
CALAMARI FRITTI WITH SPANISH TOMATO SAUCE
Prepared squid
Canola oil for deep frying
Flour mixture
Prepared tomato sauce
Lemon wedges

HAZELNUT CHOCOLATE TORTA WITH WHIPPED CREAM
Butter and flour to coat springform pan
9 ounces bittersweet chocolate
2 cups hazelnuts, chopped
18 tablespoons butter (2 sticks plus 2 tablespoons)
1 ⅓ cups sugar
6 eggs
Whipped cream
Fruit coulis

5:30 TO 6:00 PM	GUESTS ARRIVE
	Read recipes and Team Plan.
6:00 TO 7:00 PM	FINISH PREPARING APPETIZERS AND ENJOY WHILE YOU COOK
6:15 TO 6:30	CALAMARI FRITTI WITH SPANISH TOMATO SAUCE • Fry calamari. Serve.
7:30 TO 7:30 PM	ENJOY SOUP
7:30 TO 8:30	HAZELNUT CHOCOLATE TORTA • Prepare batter. • Bake and chill.
8:30 TO 9:30 PM	ENJOY ENTRÉE
9:30 TO 9:45	• Serve Hazelnut Chocolate Torta. (Team C will assist with serving dessert.)
9:45 PM	ENJOY DESSERT

HANDMADE
pasta with
HOMEMADE SAUCES

This cooking event captures the spirit of the Italian kitchen as your guests fall in love with the traditional art of hand-making pasta. You and your guests will make the dough from scratch the way the Italian grandmothers have done it for centuries. Then you will roll the dough into thin sheets with a pasta machine. Using a ravioli mold, you will make two types of ravioli: savory three-cheese and spicy Italian sausage and veal. ❧ This is a fun, but messy, experience so be sure your guests wear their aprons! Remember that fresh pasta only requires three minutes of cooking to reach the perfect *al dente* consistency. Serve the ravioli with a robust Marinara Fresca sauce and fragrant Basil Pesto. ❧ Start the night off with freshly baked focaccia, an antipasto platter, and Gorgonzola bread—a perfect sweet-and-savory combination of Gorgonzola, pear slices and walnuts. Everyone can enjoy the appetizers while making the pasta. A good Italian Chianti pairs well with the appetizers and with the pasta course. ❧ The meal will be topped off with a light homemade lemon gelato garnished with berries, to which you can add a biscotti or sugar cookie. ❧ Your guests will want to repeat this experience at home with their families!

menu

APPETIZERS

Gorgonzola Bread

Antipasto Platter

Focaccia with Dipping Oil

SALAD

Caesar Salad with
Roasted Garlic Anchovy Dressing

ENTRÉE

Italian Sausage and Veal Ravioli
Three-Cheese Ravioli

Marinara Fresca
Basil Pesto

Green Beans with Basil

DESSERT

Lemon Gelato with Berries

Biscotti or Sugar Cookie (optional)

MENU FOR EIGHT

Four Teams of Two
Team A
Team B
Team C
Team D
Total Preparation Time
Before Main Course
2 ½ Hours

The host prepares the appetizers for guests to enjoy.

gorgonzola bread

(RECIPE FROM LISÉ ZONDLER)

1	French baguette, sliced into ¼" slices
¼	cup extra virgin olive oil
2	pears, peeled, cored, and sliced
8	ounces Gorgonzola cheese
1	cup walnuts, chopped

Prepare the Gorgonzola bread approximately 30 minutes before guests arrive.

HOST **1. *Prepare Gorgonzola bread.***

Preheat oven to 350°.

Arrange baguette slices in a single layer on a baking sheet.

Brush the top of each slice with olive oil.

Place 1 or 2 slices of pear on each slice of bread.

Crumble Gorgonzola cheese on each slice. Sprinkle with chopped walnuts.

Bake 12 to 15 minutes in the preheated oven or until pears are browned and the cheese has started to melt.

antipasto platter

Fresh peppers, cut in strips

Scallions

Red roasted peppers

Pepperoncini

Green olives

Black olives

Roasted eggplant

Grape tomatoes

Marinated artichoke hearts, drained

Imported sharp provolone, sliced

Buffalo mozzarella on basil leaves

Any other Italian cheeses

Genoa salami, sliced very thin

Hard dry salami, sliced very thin

Pepperoni, sliced very thin

Prosciutto, sliced very thin

Host to prepare up to 4 hours ahead. Cover with plastic wrap and refrigerate.

HOST **1. *Arrange antipasto platter.***

Attractively arrange any combination of the listed ingredients on a large platter.

A splash of lemon juice or balsamic vinaigrette can be added.

focaccia

1⅛ cups warm water

3 cups bread flour

1½ tablespoons dry milk

1 teaspoon kosher salt

1½ tablespoons olive oil

2 tablespoons sugar

2 teaspoons active dry yeast

1 teaspoon dried Italian herbs
(rosemary, oregano or basil)

Olive oil spray

*This dough is also great for a
simple pizza crust.*

*Host prepares focaccia and dipping oil. The dough can be made early in the day
and baked approximately 1 hour before guests arrive. Alternatively, you may serve
purchased baguettes or focaccia.*

HOST   **1.** *Prepare focaccia dough.*

Put all ingredients, except herbs, into bread machine.

Run bread machine on dough setting.

When dough is finished, oil dough lightly, place in a resealable bag and
refrigerate until 1 hour before baking.

HOST   **2.** *Bake focaccia.*

Preheat to oven to 425°.

Remove dough from bag, roll out and place in a high-rimmed pizza pan
that has been sprayed with olive oil.

Sprinkle dried herbs evenly over the top of the dough.

Bake for 10 to 12 minutes until nicely browned.

Place on wooden pizza paddle and cut into sections with pizza wheel.

Serve with antipasto platter.

SERVES 8

dipping oil

¼ cup balsamic vinegar

1 cup olive oil

¼ teaspoon salt

¼ teaspoon red pepper flakes

4 cloves garlic, minced

1 tablespoon parsley,
finely chopped

Host to prepare dipping oil early in the day using high-quality oil and vinegar.

HOST   **1.** *Prepare dipping oil.*

Combine all ingredients in a 2 cup measuring cup and whisk to combine.

Pour a quarter of the dipping oil into a shallow bowl or ramekin.

Refill as needed.

MAKES 1 ¼ CUPS

caesar salad with roasted garlic anchovy dressing

DRESSING

2	heads garlic, roasted *
½	cup Parmesan cheese, freshly grated
4	tablespoons fresh lemon juice
2	tablespoons Dijon mustard
1	teaspoon Worcestershire sauce
1	teaspoon anchovy paste

Dash of Tabasco

¾	cup olive oil

CROUTONS

½	loaf French or Vienna bread
8	tablespoons olive oil

SALAD

2	large heads Romaine lettuce
½	cup Parmesan cheese, freshly shaved

Freshly ground black pepper to taste

Host to roast 2 heads garlic early in the day.

HOST   **1. *Roast garlic.***

Heat oven to 375°. Cut off the top quarter of the heads of garlic. Drizzle both sides with 2 tablespoons olive oil. Enclose in foil and place in a loaf pan. Bake for 1 hour until soft and browned. Cool. Remove cloves from skin and reserve for dressing.

TEAM C   **2. *Prepare salad dressing.***

Put all ingredients in a food processor, except olive oil. Process until well blended.

Gradually add olive oil, while processor is running, until well incorporated. Keep at room temperature until ready to serve.

TEAM D   **3. *Prepare croutons.***

Heat oven to 375°. Cut bread into ¾" slices and then cut into ¾" cubes.

Spread 8 tablespoons olive oil on rimmed baking sheet and toss cubes to coat.

Bake in a single layer for 20 minutes, turning every 5 minutes or until nicely browned.

TEAM D   **4. *Prepare lettuce.***

Wash Romaine lettuce and spin dry.

Cut into 2" strips.

TEAM D   **5. *Toss and serve salad.***

Toss Romaine with dressing and croutons.

Serve on flat plates. Top with shaved Parmesan and freshly ground pepper.

SERVES 8

egg pasta dough

(1-BATCH RECIPE)

3	cups flour
4	large eggs
1	teaspoon salt
1½	tablespoons olive oil

Note: Team A and B will each make 1 batch of dough at the shared pasta station.

HOST

1. *Prepare the pasta station.*

Prepare the pasta station for 2 teams to work on pasta.

You will require a large counter area and the following tools:

- 1 rolling pin
- 2 forks
- 1 pasta machine
- knife
- ravioli mold
- plastic wrap

TEAM A & TEAM B

2. *Make pasta dough.*

Put flour on a large board or directly on the countertop. Make a well in the center.

Break the eggs into the well. Sprinkle the salt over the eggs. Add olive oil. Start slowly stirring the flour from the edge into the eggs using a fork.

Start kneading the dough when the eggs are mixed in and have absorbed more of the flour.

Knead for 10 minutes or until the dough is smooth, elastic and shiny.

Wrap the ball of dough in plastic wrap to keep it from drying out.

TEAM A & TEAM B

3. *Prepare dough for cutting.*

Cut off ¼ of the dough to run through the pasta machine. Follow the pasta machine instructions for more details, but basically run the pasta through the machine multiple times until desired thickness is reached, making long strips to fit across the ravioli form.

SERVES 8 – 12 (2 BATCHES)

ravioli

TEAM A & TEAM B

1. *Fill ravioli.*

Fill ravioli according to instructions for your pasta machine ravioli maker.

TEAM B

2. *Bring 2 large pots of water to boil.*

TEAM C

3. *Cook ravioli in batches.*

Cook in batches. Add about 2 dozen ravioli to boiling water for 3 minutes. Use a slotted spoon to remove ravioli to a bowl. Continue to cook remaining ravioli in batches.

RAVIOLI FILLINGS

Each of these filling recipes will fill 6 to 7 dozen ravioli.

italian sausage and veal filling

2	tablespoons olive oil
¼	cup shallots, finely chopped
½	pound spicy Italian sausage, casings removed
½	pound ground veal
4	ounces crimini mushrooms, washed, trimmed and finely chopped
⅓	cup bread crumbs
½	cup heavy cream
2	eggs
2	tablespoons Italian parsley, chopped
1	teaspoon salt
½	teaspoon freshly ground black pepper

TEAM C   **1.** *Prepare meat and mushrooms.*

Heat oil in skillet and sauté shallots until lightly browned. Add sausage and cook until light brown (4 to 5 minutes). Add veal and cook another 4 minutes. Add mushrooms and cook until meat and mushrooms are fully cooked (another 4 to 5 min). Use a slotted spoon to remove meat mixture to a plate lined with paper towels. Drain.

TEAM C   **2.** *Combine ingredients.*

Combine the drained meat, bread crumbs, cream, eggs, parsley, salt and pepper in a large bowl.

TEAM C   **3.** *Chill.*

Cover and chill until ready to fill ravioli.

three-cheese filling

1	15-ounce container ricotta cheese
⅓	cup Parmesan cheese, freshly grated
3	large cloves garlic, crushed
1½	teaspoons salt
½	teaspoon black pepper
2	tablespoons Italian parsley, finely chopped
¼	pound mozzarella, finely diced
3	large egg yolks

TEAM D   **1.** *Prepare cheese filling.*

Mix all ingredients in a large bowl, incorporating the egg yokes one at a time.

TEAM D   **2.** *Chill.*

Cover and chill until ready to fill ravioli.

marinara fresca

1 28-ounce can Italian plum tomatoes
6 cloves garlic, crushed
1 teaspoon salt
½ teaspoon freshly ground black pepper
½ cup olive oil
3 tablespoons basil, cut across leaves into thin strips

TEAM D **1.** *Prepare marinara fresca.*

Add tomatoes, garlic, salt and pepper to bowl of food processor.

Process until tomatoes are chopped and ingredients are combined.

Continue to process while adding the olive oil until well incorporated.

Simmer in a small saucepan for 15 to 20 minutes. Reheat when ready to serve. Remove from heat and stir in the basil.

MAKES 3 CUPS

basil pesto

4 ½ cups loosely packed fresh basil, stems removed
3 large cloves garlic, crushed
¼ cup pine nuts
½ cup Parmesan cheese, freshly grated
1 teaspoon salt
½ teaspoon black pepper
¾ cup extra virgin olive oil

TEAM D **1.** *Prepare pesto.*

Add all ingredients except olive oil to the bowl of a food processor. Process until finely chopped. Continue to process while adding the olive oil until well incorporated.

Keep pesto at room temperature until ready to serve.

MAKES 2 ½ CUPS

green beans with basil

2 pounds green beans, washed and trimmed
10 basil leaves, cut across leaves into thin strips
Salt to taste

TEAM A **1.** *Prepare green beans.*

Bring water to boil in a steamer pot.

Place green beans in steamer basket and steam for 10 minutes.

Drain immediately to stop cooking.

Toss the green beans with the basil, season with salt and transfer to a serving bowl.

SERVES 8

lemon gelato

1   cup lemon juice,
     freshly squeezed

1   cup sugar

1 ½ cups heavy cream

1 ½ cups half and half

Zest of 1 lemon

Berries for garnish

TEAM C   **1.** *Prepare gelato mixture and chill.*

Heat the lemon juice in a medium saucepan and add the sugar. Stir over medium heat until sugar is completely dissolved. Cool.

Add the cream, half and half and lemon zest. Chill for 2 hours.

TEAM B   **2.** *Freeze gelato.*

Freeze in ice cream freezer, following directions provided. This will take approximately 40 minutes. Remove and place in a bowl with a lid and continue freezing in freezer until ready to serve.

TEAM B   **3.** *Serve dessert.*

Scoop gelato into small bowls and garnish with berries.

SERVES 8

master PLAN

host preparation

Follow *Host Prep Guidelines* on page 17.

For this menu, follow the **HOST** instructions for the following recipes:

Early in the day	*Egg Pasta Dough* (pasta stations)
Early in the day	*Caesar Salad* (roast garlic)
Early in the day	*Focaccia* (prepare dough)
Early in the day	*Dipping Oil*
Up to 4 hours ahead . . .	*Antipasto Platter*
1 hour ahead.	*Focaccia* (bake)
30 minutes ahead	*Gorgonzola Bread*

- Freeze cylinder of ice cream maker several days in advance. Review instructions for your machine.

5:30 TO 6:00 PM	GUESTS ARRIVE – HOST PROVIDES GUEST ORIENTATION – PAGE 17			
	TEAM A	**TEAM B**	**TEAM C**	**TEAM D**
6:00 TO 7:30 PM	ENJOY APPETIZERS WHILE YOU COOK			
6:00 TO 6:30	• Make pasta dough. • Prepare dough for cutting.	• Make pasta dough. • Prepare dough for cutting.	• Prepare gelato mixture and chill.	• Prepare cheese filling.
6:30 TO 7:00	• Fill cheese ravioli. (Team D makes filling.)	• Fill Italian sausage and veal ravioli. (Team C makes filling.)	• Prepare Italian sausage and veal filling.	• Prepare Marinara Fresca. • Prepare Basil Pesto.
7:00 TO 7:30		• Bring 2 large pots of water to boil. (Team C will cook ravioli.)	• Prepare salad dressing.	(Team C prepares salad dressing.) • Prepare croutons. • Prepare lettuce. • Toss and serve salad.
7:30 TO 8:00 PM	ENJOY SALAD			
8:00 TO 8:30	• Prepare green beans.	(Team C prepared and chilled gelato mixture.) • Freeze gelato.	• Cook ravioli in batches.	
8:30 TO 9:15 PM	ENJOY ENTRÉE			
9:15 TO 9:30	• Prepare coffee and serve.	• Serve dessert.		
9:30 PM	ENJOY DESSERT			

WORKSTATION:
Pasta station (includes tools)
Counter area
Stovetop

TOOLS:
Teaspoons (2)
Steamer pot
Cutting board
Knife
Large bowl

INGREDIENTS:
EGG PASTA DOUGH
3   cups flour
4   large eggs
1   teaspoon salt
1 ½ tablespoons olive oil

GREEN BEANS
WITH BASIL
2   pounds green beans, washed and trimmed
10   basil leaves, cut into thin strips
Salt to taste

5:30 TO 6:00 PM	GUESTS ARRIVE
	Read recipes and Team Plan.
6:00 TO 7:30 PM	ENJOY APPETIZERS WHILE YOU COOK
6:00 TO 6:30	EGG PASTA DOUGH • Make pasta dough. • Prepare dough for cutting.
6:30 TO 7:30	CHEESE RAVIOLI • Fill cheese ravioli. (Team D makes filling.)
7:30 TO 8:00 PM	ENJOY SALAD
8:00 TO 8:30	GREEN BEANS WITH BASIL • Prepare green beans.
8:30 TO 9:15 PM	ENJOY ENTRÉE
9:15 TO 9:30	• Prepare coffee and serve.
9:30 PM	ENJOY DESSERT

HANDMADE PASTA WITH HOMEMADE SAUCES

TEAM B

WORKSTATION:

Pasta station (includes tools)

Counter area

Stovetop

TOOLS:

Teaspoons (2)

Large pots for pasta (2)

Ice cream freezer

Bowl with cover for ice cream

Large spoon

INGREDIENTS:

EGG PASTA DOUGH

3 cups flour

4 large eggs

1 teaspoon salt

1 ½ tablespoons olive oil

LEMON GELATO

Berries for garnish

5:30 TO 6:00 PM	**GUESTS ARRIVE**
	Read recipes and Team Plan.
6:00 TO 7:30 PM	**ENJOY APPETIZERS WHILE YOU COOK**
6:00 TO 6:30	EGG PASTA DOUGH • Make pasta dough. • Prepare dough for cutting.
6:30 TO 7:00	ITALIAN SAUSAGE AND VEAL RAVIOLI • Fill Italian sausage and veal ravioli. (Team C makes Italian sausage and veal filling.)
7:00 TO 7:30	RAVIOLI • Bring two large pots of water to boil. (Team C will cook ravioli when ready for pasta course.)
7:30 TO 8:00 PM	**ENJOY SALAD**
8:00 TO 8:30	LEMON GELATO (Team C prepared and chilled Gelato mixture.) • Freeze Gelato.
8:30 TO 9:15 PM	**ENJOY ENTRÉE**
9:15 TO 9:30	• Serve dessert.
9:30 PM	**ENJOY DESSERT**

WORKSTATION:
Counter area
Stovetop

TOOLS:
Cutting board
Knife
Juicer
Measuring cups
Measuring spoons
Medium saucepan
Skillet
Large plate with paper towel
Large bowl for filling
Large bowl
Grater
Spoon
Small food processor

Large pasta pots (2)
Slotted spoon

INGREDIENTS:
LEMON GELATO
1   cup lemon juice, freshly squeezed
1   cup sugar
1 ½ cups heavy cream
1 ½ cups half and half
Zest of 1 lemon

ITALIAN SAUSAGE AND VEAL FILLING
2   tablespoons olive oil
¼   cup shallots, finely chopped
½   pound spicy Italian sausage, casings removed
½   pound ground veal
4   ounces crimini mushrooms, washed, trimmed and finely chopped
⅓   cup bread crumbs
½   cup heavy cream
2   eggs
2   tablespoons Italian parsley, chopped
1   teaspoons salt
½   teaspoon freshly ground black pepper

ROASTED GARLIC ANCHOVY DRESSING
2   heads roasted garlic
½   cup Parmesan cheese, freshly grated
4   tablespoons fresh lemon juice
2   tablespoons Dijon mustard
1   teaspoon Worcestershire sauce
1   teaspoon anchovy paste
Dash of Tabasco
¾   cup olive oil

5:30 TO 6:00 PM	**GUESTS ARRIVE**
	Read recipes and Team Plan.
6:00 TO 7:30 PM	**ENJOY APPETIZERS WHILE YOU COOK**
6:00 TO 6:30	**LEMON GELATO** • Prepare gelato mixture and chill.
6:30 TO 7:00	**ITALIAN SAUSAGE AND VEAL FILLING** • Prepare meat and mushrooms. • Combine ingredients. • Chill.
7:00 TO 7:30	**CAESAR SALAD WITH ROASTED GARLIC ANCHOVY DRESSING** • Prepare salad dressing.
7:30 TO 8:00 PM	**ENJOY SALAD**
8:00 TO 8:30	**RAVIOLI** • Cook ravioli in batches.
8:30 TO 9:15 PM	**ENJOY ENTRÉE**
9:30 PM	**ENJOY DESSERT**

HANDMADE PASTA WITH HOMEMADE SAUCES

WORKSTATION:
Counter area
Stovetop
Oven

TOOLS:
Large bowl
Spoon
Plastic wrap
Food processor
Small saucepan (marinara)
Cutting board
Knife
Garlic press
Measuring cups
Grater
Measuring spoons
Food processor

Bread knife
Baking sheet
Lettuce spinner

INGREDIENTS:
CHEESE FILLING
1 15-ounce container ricotta cheese
⅓ cup Parmesan, freshly grated
3 large cloves garlic, crushed
1½ teaspoons salt
½ teaspoon black pepper
2 tablespoons Italian parsley, finely chopped
¼ pound mozzarella, finely diced
3 large egg yolks

MARINARA FRESCA
1 28-ounce can Italian plum tomatoes
6 cloves garlic, crushed
1 teaspoon salt
½ teaspoon freshly ground black pepper
½ cup olive oil
3 tablespoons basil, cut into thin strips

BASIL PESTO
4½ cups loosely packed fresh basil
3 large garlic cloves, crushed
¼ cup pine nuts
½ cup Parmesan cheese, freshly grated

1 teaspoon salt
½ teaspoon black pepper
¾ cup extra virgin olive oil

CROUTONS
½ loaf of French or Vienna bread
8 tablespoons olive oil

SALAD
2 large heads Romaine
½ cup Parmesan cheese, freshly shaved
Freshly ground black pepper to taste

5:30 TO 6:00 PM	GUESTS ARRIVE

Read recipes and Team Plan.

6:00 TO 7:30 PM	ENJOY APPETIZERS WHILE YOU COOK

6:00 TO 6:30	THREE CHEESE FILLING • Prepare cheese filling. • Chill.
6:30 TO 7:00	MARINARA FRESCA • Prepare Marinara Fresca. BASIL PESTO • Prepare pesto.
7:00 TO 7:30	CAESAR SALAD WITH ROASTED GARLIC ANCHOVY DRESSING (Team C prepares salad dressing.) • Prepare croutons. • Prepare lettuce. • Toss and serve salad.

7:30 TO 8:00 PM	ENJOY SALAD
8:30 TO 9:15 PM	ENJOY ENTRÉE
9:30 PM	ENJOY DESSERT

AUTHENTIC TASTES OF
indonesia

Indonesian cuisine is as diverse as the 6,000 inhabited islands that constitute this Southeast Asian country. This menu showcases the warm, pungent flavors of coriander, turmeric, cumin and ginger in several authentic dishes. To streamline preparation, the host prepares a spice-paste blend ahead of time. The paste is then used in the Lumpiah (spring rolls) filled with thin shards of carrots, cabbage and bean sprouts. Spice paste flavors the Soto Ayam (chicken soup) that is fragrant with lemon grass, and is also used to give a golden hue to the Nasi Goreng (fried rice). Satés or Satays—skewered spicy beef, chicken or shrimp—are very popular in Indonesia. The accompanying creamy peanut sauce has a bit of punch with a jalapeño kick. A colorful stir-fry of carrots and snow peas rounds out the meal. And a simple tropical dessert of pineapple and kiwi makes a refreshing finale. Be sure to use bright colors on your table, and consider using banana leaves to line your serving dishes for an additional touch of authenticity.

menu

APPETIZERS

Bowls of Assorted Nuts, Dried Fruit and Coconut

Lumpiah (Indonesian Spring Rolls) with Kecap Manis for Dipping

SOUP

Soto Ayam (Chicken Soup)

ENTRÉE

Satés of Beef, Chicken, and Shrimp with Spicy Peanut Sauce

Nasi Goreng (Indonesian Fried Rice)

Carrot and Snow Pea Stir Fry

DESSERT

Pineapple and Kiwi Boat

MENU FOR EIGHT

Four Teams of Two
Team A
Team B
Team C
Team D
Total Preparation Time
Before Main Course
2 Hours

Authentic Tastes of Indonesia
Cook the Part
Hosted by Susan Dubé
March 3, 2011

Starters
Bowls of Assorted nuts, dried fruit and
coconut
Lumpiah (Indonesian Spring Rolls) with
Kecap Manis for Dipping

Soup
Soto Ayam (Chicken Soup)

Entrees
Satés of Shrimp, Chicken and Filet with
Spicy Peanut Sauce
Nasi Goreng (Indonesian Fried Rice)
Stir Fry of Carrots and Snow Peas

Dessert
Pineapple and Kiwi Boat

bowls of assorted nuts, dried fruit and coconut

Variety of nuts
Variety of dried fruit
Shredded coconut

Any local organic food market is a great place to find nuts and dried fruit for this simple appetizer.

HOST

1. *Prepare bowls of nuts and dried fruit.*

Mix nuts, dried fruit and shredded coconut. Serve in small attractive bowls.

lumpiah (indonesian spring rolls)

2	tablespoons canola oil
5	medium carrots, peeled, julienned
½	head cabbage, shredded*
12	ounces bean sprouts
3	tablespoons spice paste
1	teaspoon salt
½	teaspoon pepper

Thin rice paper wrappers (these are round and can be found at Asian markets)

*Cut cabbage in half and remove core.
Slice very thinly or use mandolin to shred.

TEAM A

1. *Prepare filling.*

Heat oil in a large skillet. Add the carrots and cabbage and sauté for 3 minutes. Add the sprouts and continue cooking for 2 additional minutes. Add the spice paste, salt and pepper and mix well. Cook for an additional 3 minutes until vegetables are soft but still somewhat crisp. Remove and set aside to cool.

TEAM A

2. *Fill the wrappers.*

Soak a wrapper until limp (1 minute) in a bowl of cool water. Lay wrapper on a flat surface. Place 3 tablespoons of the filling on the end of each wrapper and tightly roll the wrapper around the contents, as if making a burrito. Moisten at seam; press to close. Lay them on a plate, cover with a moist paper towel and refrigerate until ready to serve. Cut each in half diagonally; serve with the kecap manis as a dipping sauce.

MAKES 16 ROLLS

The Host should prepare the following items.
These can be made up to 1 week ahead and refrigerated until ready to use.

spice paste

½	teaspoon coriander seeds
1 ½	teaspoons turmeric powder
1	teaspoon cumin seeds
½	teaspoon cayenne pepper
½	teaspoon ground black pepper
1	teaspoon salt
½	teaspoon chili powder
2	large shallots, chopped
6	large garlic cloves, crushed
1	2" piece of fresh ginger, peeled and sliced

Juice of ½ lime

3	tablespoons water

The spice paste is used for the Lumpiah (Indonesian Spring Rolls), Soto Ayam (Chicken Soup) and the Nasi Goreng (Fried Rice).

HOST **1.** *Prepare spice paste.*
Process all ingredients in food processor until a paste forms.

MAKES ¾ CUP PASTE

kecap manis

½	cup boiling water
1	cup brown sugar
1	cup soy sauce
1	1" piece peeled and chopped ginger
4	garlic cloves, crushed

Juice of ½ lime

The kecap manis is served with the lumpiah and is used for the marinade for the satés.

HOST **1.** *Prepare kecap manis.*
Make a simple syrup of the boiling water and brown sugar. Add other ingredients. Pour into a jar with a lid and reserve until needed. Strain and use.

MAKES 2 CUPS

soto ayam (chicken soup)

2   organic, skinless, boneless chicken breasts (about 1¼ pounds), cut into bite-size cubes

3   tablespoons peanut oil

4   tablespoons spice paste

1   stalk lemon grass (cut into 3 pieces)

2   32-ounce boxes organic chicken broth

3   cups water

1   teaspoon salt

2   cups shredded cabbage

2   cups bean sprouts

1   small package of glass noodles (6 ounces)

2   hard-boiled eggs (cut into 4 wedges each)

½   cup chopped green onions (green part included)

TEAM C

1. *Prepare soup.*

Cube chicken as indicated. Heat the peanut oil in a large stock pot. Add the cubed chicken and sauté until chicken is lightly browned and cooked. Remove the chicken and reserve. Add the spice paste to the pot and sauté until well blended with chicken drippings.

Trim the stem end of the lemon grass stalk and remove any coarse outer layers. Cut into 3 pieces. Add the lemon grass, chicken broth, water and salt to the pot and bring to boil. Simmer for 10 minutes and add the chicken. Simmer an additional 30 to 40 minutes. Remove lemon grass.

TEAM B

2. *Finish soup.*

Add the cabbage and sprouts to the stock pot and cook for an additional 10 minutes. Soak and drain the glass noodles (according to package directions). Snip through noodles with scissors to make shorter strands; add to the soup. Heat through.

TEAM B

3. *Serve soup.*

Ladle the soup into bowls; add one wedge of egg to each bowl and garnish with the chopped green onion.

SERVES 8

satés of beef, chicken and shrimp with spicy peanut sauce

SATÉS

1½ pounds filet mignon, cut into 3" strips across the grain, ½" wide, ½" thick

1½ pounds boneless, skinless chicken breasts cut into ½" strips

24 large shrimp, peeled, deveined, tails on

36 bamboo skewers, soaked in water for at least 1 hour

Banana leaves for serving décor

MARINADE

1 cup kecap manis

4 garlic cloves, crushed

Juice of 1 lime

1 teaspoon dry coriander

½ teaspoon chili powder

1 teaspoon salt

SPICY PEANUT SAUCE

1 cup creamy peanut butter

1 14½ ounce can organic chicken broth

Juice of ½ lime

2 garlic cloves, minced

2 tablespoons brown sugar

2 tablespoons soy sauce

2 tablespoons peeled, chopped fresh ginger

½ teaspoon dried crushed red pepper

1 tablespoon sesame oil

½ teaspoon chopped jalapeño

½ teaspoon cayenne pepper

TEAM D **1.** *Prepare satés.*

Cut beef and chicken into strips as indicated. Prepare shrimp as indicated.

Skewer beef, chicken and shrimp. Keep like-meat items on separate skewers to facilitate different grilling times. Place in shallow pans.

TEAM B **2.** *Prepare marinade.*

Combine all ingredients in a bowl and pour over skewered satés. Refrigerate until ready to grill or broil.

TEAM A **3.** *Prepare peanut sauce.*

Heat peanut butter in a medium-sized saucepan over medium heat. Gradually add chicken broth until well blended. Add remaining ingredients. Stir continuously until sauce begins to simmer. Simmer for 10 minutes over low heat, stirring frequently. Remove from burner, but leave in saucepan and reheat when ready to serve.

TEAM D **4.** *Grill satés.*

Heat grill to medium. Grill the skewers as follows:

Grill chicken skewers 4 to 5 minutes per side.

Grill beef skewers about 3 minutes per side for medium rare.

Grill shrimp skewers about 2 minutes per side. Cook just until they turn pink; remove from heat so as not to overcook.

SERVES 8

nasi goreng (indonesian fried rice)

2 cups long grain white rice

2 cups organic chicken broth

2 cups water

1 teaspoon salt

FRIED RICE

3 tablespoons peanut oil, divided

2 large eggs, beaten

1 cup chopped red onions

1 cup chopped carrots

2 tablespoons spice paste

4 garlic cloves, crushed

1 cup frozen peas

2 teaspoons sesame oil

2 tablespoons soy sauce

½ cup chopped green onions for garnish

Host to cook rice 1 day ahead.

HOST **1.** *Cook rice.*

Combine all ingredients in rice cooker or medium-sized saucepan. Cover and simmer rice for 20 minutes; turn off heat; cool. Refrigerate 1 day before making the fried rice.

TEAM C **2.** *Prepare fried rice.*

Heat 1 teaspoon peanut oil in a large frying pan or wok and scramble the eggs in the oil. Remove eggs. Add 1 tablespoon oil to frying pan. Fry the red onions and carrots until soft, about 5 to 7 minutes. Add the spice paste and garlic and cook for 3 more minutes. Remove and reserve the vegetables. Add remaining oil to the pan. Add the rice and mix until all the rice is coated with some of the oil. Add the frozen peas, sesame oil, soy sauce and vegetables and cook until peas are hot. Add the cooked egg to the rice and heat through. Garnish with chopped green onions.

SERVES 8

carrot and snow pea stir fry

2 tablespoons peanut oil

5 large carrots, peeled and sliced on the diagonal

3 cups snow peas, prepared*

1 jalapeño, seeded, finely minced

2 tablespoons soy sauce

2 tablespoons ginger, peeled and chopped

Juice of ½ lime

Salt to taste

* Pinch the tip of the snow pea and pull out the string that runs down the side.

TEAM B **1.** *Stir fry vegetables.*

Heat peanut oil in a large skillet or wok. Add carrots and sauté for 4 minutes. Add snow peas, jalapeño, soy sauce and ginger. Sauté until snow peas and carrots are crisp, but tender. Add lime juice and salt to taste.

SERVES 8

pineapple and kiwi boat

4   ripe kiwis
1   large ripe pineapple

This is a very simple and satisfying dessert following the many spices and flavors in this Indonesian dinner.

TEAM B   **1. *Prepare kiwis.***

Using a small knife, peel and slice the kiwis.

TEAM D   **2. *Prepare pineapple for serving.***

Cut the pineapple in half lengthwise.

Cut across the inside of each half into ½" slices. Cut around the outer edges of the pineapple to remove the slices. Cut each slice into 3 or 4 sections. Return to the open pineapple half and mix with kiwi slices.

TEAM D   **3. *Serve.***

SERVES 8

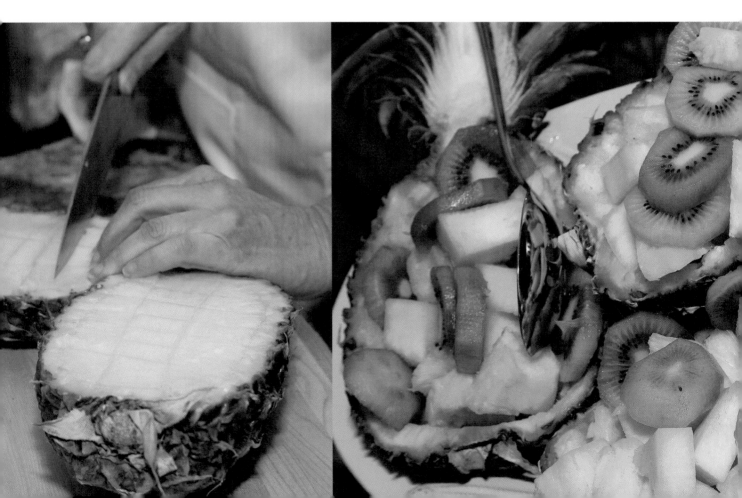

master
PLAN

host preparation

Follow *Host Prep Guidelines* on page 17.

- Prepare hard boiled eggs for soup up to a day ahead.
- Soak bamboo skewers at least one hour before grilling.

For this menu, follow the **HOST** instructions for the following recipes:

Up to 1 week ahead . . . *Spice Paste* and *Kecap Manis*

1 day ahead . . . . *Nasi Goreng* (cook rice)

1 hour ahead. . . . . . . *Bowls of Assorted Nuts, Dried Fruit and Coconut* (assemble nuts and dried fruit)

5:30 TO 6:00 PM	GUESTS ARRIVE — HOST PROVIDES GUEST ORIENTATION — PAGE 17			
	TEAM A	TEAM B	TEAM C	TEAM D
6:00 TO 7:30 PM	PREPARE APPETIZERS AND ENJOY WHILE YOU COOK			
6:00 TO 7:00	• Prepare filling for spring rolls. • Fill the wrappers.	• Prepare marinade and pour over skewered satés. • Prepare kiwis. (Give to Team D.)	• Prepare soup.	• Prepare satés.
7:00 TO 7:30	• Prepare peanut sauce.	• Finish soup. • Serve soup.		• Prepare pineapple for serving. (Get kiwis from Team B.)
7:30 TO 8:00 PM	ENJOY SOUP			
8:00 TO 8:30		• Stir fry vegetables.	• Prepare fried rice.	• Grill satés.
8:30 TO 9:30 PM	ENJOY ENTRÉE			
9:30 TO 9:45	• Prepare coffee and serve.			• Serve dessert.
9:45 PM	ENJOY DESSERT			

WORKSTATION:
Counter area
Stovetop

TOOLS:
Measuring spoons
Large skillet
Spatula
Spoon
Paper towels
Measuring cup
Saucepan
Wooden spoon

INGREDIENTS:
LUMPIAH (INDONESIAN SPRING ROLLS)
2 tablespoons canola oil
5 medium carrots, peeled, julienned
½ head cabbage, shredded
12 ounces bean sprouts
3 tablespoons spice paste
1 teaspoon salt
½ teaspoon pepper
Thin rice paper wrappers

SPICY PEANUT SAUCE
1 cup creamy peanut butter
1 14 ½ ounce can organic chicken broth
Juice of ½ lime
2 garlic cloves, minced
2 tablespoons brown sugar
2 tablespoons soy sauce
2 tablespoons peeled, chopped fresh ginger
½ teaspoon dried crushed red pepper
1 tablespoon sesame oil
½ teaspoon chopped jalapeño
½ teaspoon cayenne pepper

5:30 TO 6:00 PM	GUESTS ARRIVE
	Read recipes and Team Plan.
6:00 TO 7:30 PM	**PREPARE APPETIZERS AND ENJOY WHILE YOU COOK**
6:00 TO 7:00	LUMPIAH (INDONESIAN SPRING ROLLS) • Prepare filling. • Fill the wrappers.
7:00 TO 7:30	SPICY PEANUT SAUCE • Prepare peanut sauce.
7:30 TO 8:00 PM	ENJOY SOUP
8:30 TO 9:30 PM	ENJOY ENTRÉE
9:30 TO 9:45	• Prepare coffee and serve.
9:45 PM	ENJOY DESSERT

AUTHENTIC TASTES OF INDONESIA

WORKSTATION:
Counter area
Stovetop

TOOLS:
Small bowl
Measuring cup
Measuring spoons
Small knife
Cutting board
Soaking bowl
Scissors
Ladle
Large frying pan or wok
Spatula

INGREDIENTS:

MARINADE
1   cup kecap manis
4   garlic cloves, crushed
Juice of one lime
1   teaspoon dry coriander
½ teaspoon chili powder
1   teaspoon salt

**PINEAPPLE AND
KIWI BOAT**
4   ripe kiwis

**SOTO AYAM
(CHICKEN SOUP)**
2   cups shredded cabbage
1   cup bean sprouts
1   small package of glass
    noodles (6 ounces)
2   hard-boiled eggs (cut
    into 4 wedges each)
½ cup chopped green
    onions

**CARROT AND SNOW PEA
STIR FRY**
2   tablespoons peanut oil
5   large carrots, peeled
    and sliced on the diagonal
3   cups snow peas,
    prepared
1   jalapeño, seeded and
    finely minced
2   tablespoons soy sauce
2   tablespoons ginger,
    peeled and chopped
Juice of ½ lime
Salt to taste

5:30 TO 6:00 PM	**GUESTS ARRIVE**
	Read recipes and Team Plan.
6:00 TO 7:30 PM	**PREPARE APPETIZERS AND ENJOY WHILE YOU COOK**
6:00 TO 7:00	MARINADE • Prepare marinade. PINEAPPLE AND KIWI BOAT • Prepare kiwis. (Give to Team D.)
7:00 TO 7:30	SOTO AYAM (CHICKEN SOUP) • Finish soup. • Serve soup.
7:30 TO 8:00 PM	**ENJOY SOUP**
8:00 TO 8:30	CARROT AND SNOW PEA STIR FRY • Stir fry vegetables.
8:30 TO 9:30 PM	**ENJOY ENTRÉE**
9:45 PM	**ENJOY DESSERT**

WORKSTATION:

Counter area

Stovetop

TOOLS:

Knife

Cutting board

Large stock pot

Spatula

Measuring spoons

Measuring cup

Large frying pan or wok

Plate

Spatula

INGREDIENTS:

SOTO AYAM (CHICKEN SOUP)

- 2 organic, skinless, boneless chicken breasts (about 1 ¼ pounds), cut into bite size cubes
- 3 tablespoons peanut oil
- 4 tablespoons spice paste
- 1 stalk lemon grass (cut into 3 pieces)
- 2 32-ounce boxes organic chicken broth
- 3 cups water
- 1 teaspoon salt

NASI GORENG (INDONESIAN FRIED RICE)

- 3 tablespoons peanut oil, divided
- 2 large eggs, beaten
- 1 cup chopped red onions
- 1 cup chopped carrots
- 2 tablespoons spice paste
- 4 garlic cloves, crushed
- 1 cup frozen peas
- 2 teaspoons sesame oil
- 2 tablespoons soy sauce
- ½ cup chopped green onions for garnish

5:30 TO 6:00 PM	**GUESTS ARRIVE**
	Read recipes and Team Plan.
6:00 TO 7:30 PM	**PREPARE APPETIZERS AND ENJOY WHILE YOU COOK**
6:00 TO 7:00	SOTO AYAM (CHICKEN SOUP) • Prepare soup.
7:30 TO 8:00 PM	**ENJOY SOUP**
8:00 TO 8:30	INDONESIAN FRIED RICE (NASI GORENG) • Prepare fried rice.
8:30 TO 9:30 PM	**ENJOY ENTRÉE**
9:45 PM	**ENJOY DESSERT**

AUTHENTIC TASTES OF INDONESIA

WORKSTATION:
Counter area
Grill

TOOLS:
Cutting board
Large knife
Small knife
Bamboo skewers
Shallow pans
Grill racks
Grill tongs

INGREDIENTS:
SATÉS BEEF, CHICKEN
AND SHRIMP

1 ½ pounds filet mignon, cut
  into 3" strips across the
  grain, ½" wide,
  ½" thick

1 ½ pounds boneless skin-
  less chicken breasts, cut
  into ½" strips

24 large shrimp, peeled,
  deveined, tails on

36 bamboo skewers,
  soaked in water for at
  least one hour

Banana leaves for serving

PINEAPPLE AND
KIWI BOAT

1 large ripe pineapple

5:30 TO 6:00 PM	GUESTS ARRIVE
	Read recipes and Team Plan.
6:00 TO 7:30 PM	**PREPARE APPETIZERS AND ENJOY WHILE YOU COOK**
6:00 TO 7:00	SATÉS • Prepare satés.
7:00 TO 7:30	PINEAPPLE AND KIWI BOAT • Prepare pineapple for serving. (Get kiwis from Team B.)
7:30 TO 8:00 PM	**ENJOY SALAD**
8:00 TO 8:30	SATÉS • Grill satés.
8:30 TO 9:30 PM	**ENJOY ENTRÉE**
9:30 TO 9:45	PINEAPPLE AND KIWI BOAT • Serve.
9:45 PM	**ENJOY DESSERT**